CHRIST IN THE LIGHT OF THE CHRISTIAN-JEWISH DIALOGUE

John Pawlikowski

A Stimulus Book

Paulist Press ■ New York ■ Ramsey

Library of Congress
Catalog Card Number: 81-83186

ISBN: 0-8091-2416-5

Published by Paulist Press
545 Island Road, Ramsey, N.J. 07446

Printed and bound in the
United States of America

Contents

dedicated to
James Parkes,
J. Coert Rylaarsdam
& Jules Isaac,
who first led me to rethink
the Christian-Jewish relationship

1
Introduction: Why Christology?

Positive Advance Despite Frustration

The Christian-Jewish dialogue has evidenced significant development in the decade or more since Vatican Council II's historic declaration on the Church and the Jewish people. Prompted by this declaration, by similar declarations from various ecumenical and denominational Protestant groups, and by the 1975 Vatican Guidelines for Catholic-Jewish Relations, scholars and educators have focused new attention on various aspects of the Jewish-Christian relationship.[1] Recently Orthodox Christianity, while not issuing any official statements akin to the Catholic and Protestant declarations (though, as a member of the World Council of Churches, it is a signatory to WCC statements), has begun to explore its attitudes towards Judaism in greater depth. The same may be said for the Evangelical Christian community.[2]

The principal thrust of the early encounter between Jews and Christians was the elimination of classical antisemitic stereotypes of Jews, especially the so-called "deicide charge." As a result of textbook studies undertaken by Christian groups in various countries, some dramatic changes have appeared during the last several years, although it is necessary to caution that not all problems have yet been resolved.[3] Serious efforts have also been made to tackle stereotypes of Jews that are enforced through the liturgy, with special focus on Lent and Holy Week. Professor John Townsend of the Episcopal Seminary at Harvard has prepared an interpolated text of the Passion narrative that eliminates many of the traditional problem areas.[4] The Secretariat for Catholic-Jewish Relations in Washington has issued guidelines for homilists, and several local dioceses such as Los Angeles have initiated creative responses to the problem of handling scriptural texts used in the liturgy that appear to denigrate

1

Jews. Attempts have also been made to develop liturgies commemorating the Holocaust. This movement was given new emphasis by the 1978 proclamation by President Carter of an official national day of remembrance in the United States for the Holocaust victims.[5]

In addition to the above more popularly directed activities, a small but dedicated group of Christian scholars such as A. Roy Eckardt, Rosemary Ruether, Gerard Sloyan, Monika Hellwig, Gregory Baum and others have begun to explore the theological dimensions of the Christian-Jewish dialogue. Very recently they have been joined in this endeavor in a beginning way by some major systematicians such as Jürgen Moltmann, Hans Küng and Edward Schillebeeckx.

The growing realization of the significance of the Holocaust has engendered further explorations of the Christian-Jewish relationship by theologians. Among the leaders here are such figures as Franklin Sherman, Marcel Dubois, Michael Ryan and Franklin Littell. On the Jewish side there has been some advance as well. The starting point for Jews, however, is quite different since Christianity is not integral to the self-definition of Judaism in the same way as Judaism is to Christianity. The history of persecution of Jews by Christians "in the name of Christ" further complicates the Jewish response. However, a major textbook study of Jewish attitudes toward Christianity was undertaken at Dropsie College in Philadelphia during the same period as the Catholic and Protestant studies,[6] while in Israel major textbook revamping produced an appraisal of Jesus' connection to the Jewish community of his time that was positive enough to elicit protests from the ultra-orthodox factions who insisted that the matter be debated in Parliament.[7] Additionally, several Jewish scholars have begun a re-examination of Jesus from a Jewish perspective and the possible meaning that Christianity might carry for contemporary Jewish religious expression. David Flusser, Samuel Sandmel, Eugene Borowitz, Irving Greenberg, David Hartman, Ellis Rivkin and Shemaryahu Talmon are some prominent names in this effort.

Tensions remain between the two faith communities. There is little doubt about this. The memory of Christian antisemitism, and of Auschwitz in particular, continues in the Jewish community. The Middle East wars of 1967 and 1973 and what many Jews perceived as an overwhelming Christian silence in the face of a threat to continued Jewish survival affected the mood of the dialogue. Yet overall there is clear evidence of steady progress toward a significant reversal in the way the two faith communities have depicted each other for centuries.

Christological Restatement a Key

I have had the privilege of sharing in the enrichment and frustration of the dialogue for well over a decade. During this period a slow but steady conviction began to emerge in me that no lasting resolution of the historic Christian-Jewish tension is possible unless the Church is ready to significantly rethink its traditional interpretation of Christology. Rosemary Ruether's writings, especially her volume *Faith and Fratricide*,[8] have brought the issue to a head for me. The positives and negatives of Ruether's approach will be examined in a subsequent chapter. But for me there remains little doubt about the need for a profound re-examination of the Christological question if the Church is to construct a solid, positive theology of Judaism in our time.

This theology will have to abandon some of the classic Christian formulations that Christ has fulfilled the messianic prophecies of the Hebrew Scriptures and inaugurated the expected messianic age. On the other hand, neither will it be satisfactory to simply reduce the experience of Christ to one among many experiences of messianic hope, as Ruether appears to do, nor merely to understand Christianity as Judaism for the Gentiles, a thesis being developed of late by Paul Van Buren and others. Unless Christianity is able to articulate some unique features in the revelation of Christ, then it should fold up as a major world religion. That may be too bluntly stated, but there is no purpose in disguising the fact that Christianity's continued meaningfulness as a faith community depends on seeing dimensions of religious significance within it that are not present in other faith expressions and experiences. And the Christ event, however interpreted by different churches and scholars, stands at the very heart of Christian faith expression.

This point has been further reinforced for me with the intensified discussions within Christianity about the evangelization of Jews. In the Protestant community where organizationally such efforts have traditionally carried a greater priority than in Catholicism or Orthodoxy, the debate erupted in connection with an article published by Rabbi Balfour Brickner, then the Director of Interreligious Affairs for the Union of American Hebrew Congregations and a long-time participant in the interreligious dialogue. In the journal *Worldview*, Brickner argues for a clear repudiation of proselytism on the part of the Christian churches toward the Jewish community.[9] Without such repudiation, he feels, the dialogue has little chance of further advancement.

Brickner's comments called forth reactions from several Christian leaders. In essence, all maintained that while antisemitism and coercive conversion measures are to be clearly rejected, the Church can never abandon in principle its mission to evangelize all non-Christians, including Jews. Such evangelization is at the very heart of the universal salvation and fulfillment brought about in the Christ event.[10]

A similar reaction has surfaced in some Catholic circles in regard to the publication of the study paper by Professor Tomaso Federici of San Anselmo University in Rome.[11] Even though concrete efforts to convert Jews have virtually ceased in recent years in the Catholic Church, Federici's desire to raise non-proselytism to the level of theological principle met with opposition similar to that elicited by the Brickner essay.

In his paper, originally prepared for a 1977 meeting in Venice of the Vatican's Commission for Religious Relations with the Jews and Jewish representatives, Federici unequivocally rejects all conventional missionary efforts toward the Jewish community. He does allow for witness to Jews on the part of Christians, but such witness must be given in the context of reverent dialogue where Jews have the opportunity to share their own faith experiences with members of the Church. Federici, however, fails to address the fundamental Christological issues related to the significant attitudinal change to which he is summoning the Church. As a result, the Federici paper will appear to many as just another attempt to abandon the Gospel mandate of universal evangelization.

Until such time as the Christological problem is forthrightly faced by Christians, authentic dialogue between Christians and Jews will remain problematic. There will always linger a sense of mistrust on the part of the Jewish community based on fear that dialogue is a new form of convert-making. Even more importantly, the repudiation of organized missionary campaigns directed toward Jews in a particular locality will remain almost totally a matter of goodwill and experience on the part of individual Christians, rather than an expression of sound Christian theology. Based on concrete experience the repudiation in most cases will prove timid at best, for fear that a public stand against such a campaign would seem to compromise New Testament injunctions.

Hence the necessity to directly confront the Christological issue. We must begin to lay some foundation stones for a new Christology that will preserve the uniqueness of the Christ event and at the same time will lead to a positive Christian theology of Judaism. That is this volume's ultimate goal. In the process of doing this, important attempts by Christian participants in the dialogue will be analyzed as well as the writings of several major systematicians in the Catholic and Protestant communities. Finally, the discussion will be set in the context of the experience of the Holocaust which Rabbi Irving Greenberg has rightly termed an "orienting event" that is revelatory for both contemporary Judaism and Christianity.[12]

Methodological Assumptions

A word or two about some assumptions are in order. In the first place, though I am convinced that the new Christology that needs to be developed will be forced to reject *some* traditional interpretations of the Christ event, such rejections will at least in part be based on a more accurate understanding of the Jewish context of New Testament thought than most Christians have possessed up till now. In her challenging volume *Anti-Judaism in Christian Theology*,[13] Charlotte Klein has demonstrated quite persuasively that many of the traditional Christian theological interpretations of Judaism and its relationship to the Christ event were rooted in a biblical scholarship that was seriously inaccurate in its portrayal of Second Temple Judaism. This was especially true for continental European theology, a significant point in view of the fact that until very recently that geographic area served as the principal breeding ground for Christian theological thought. Thus, in part, the new Christology will be more faithful to the New Testament than have been some of the historic interpretations.

Yet, in no way do I wish to disguise the fact that this new Christology involves as well the outright rejection of some Christological directions taken by the Christian churches. The justification for this can only be found in a dynamic interpretation of the concept of tradition as a source of revelation.

Peter Chirico has delineated such an expanded notion of tradition in an essay dealing specifically with Christian-Jewish relations. He emphasizes:

> Tradition is not the mere exegesis of Scripture but rather the understanding and expression by the community of the progressive unfolding of revelation that is taking place within it and the world at large in the course of history.[14]

Chirico goes on to argue that the content of revelation is able to develop, in fact must develop, because revelation is co-terminous with creation itself. Viewing the human person as the manifestation of the revealing activity of

God in creation, Chirico maintains that since individuals and communities have changed and developed, it follows that revelation is continually changing and developing as well throughout the course of history.

Robert Schreiter in discussing the approach to Christology of Edward Schillebeeckx and how it might affect the dialogue between Christians and Jews opens up another methodological possibility for the kind of Christological reinterpretation to be dealt with in later chapters. [15] His approach might be termed an attempt to relate the classic theological category of tradition to the insights offered by modern language analysis. Schreiter underscores Schillebeeckx's suggestion that statements about Christian fulfillment need to be read as anticipatory and proleptic instead of participatory with respect to the reign of God. Hence there is need to continually reread the classic Christian texts in the light of new experiences. Schreiter sees many of the eschatological and messianic texts of the New Testament as attempts to mediate the felt presence but equally realized absence of Jesus in the midst of his disciples. Recognizing that every religious affirmation will include an element of non-meaning, and understanding the anticipatory nature of many of the earliest Christian Christological claims, it is possible for us today to develop new insights as a result of new experiences of meaning. The living encounter with Jews and with Judaism as a faith community can provide Christians and the Church as a whole with new meaning that will require adjustment in messianic and eschatological understandings.

To my mind no adequate solution to the Christological problems vis-à-vis Judaism will be attained solely within the framework of the Bible. Hence, in principle, I think that the Catholic and Orthodox communities may have a somewhat easier time dealing with the Christological issue than traditional Protestantism with its "a scriptura sola" orientation.

I am fully aware that there are both Christian and Jewish scholars who feel that the above approach exceeds the proper limitations of the dialogue. They would insist that there is nothing wrong for either Jew or Christian to maintain the universal applicability and superiority of their respective notions of salvation. In fact, it is imperative that they do so if they are to remain faithful to their individual covenants. This school of thought would posit that hostility toward other religious groups need not be part of an authentic universalistic interpretation. It is possible for competing universalisms to stand together in love and respect without anyone repudiating their claims. The Israeli scholar Shemaryahu Talmon, long active in dialogue on an international level, encourages such an approach. Christians, Jews and other religious and ideological groups need to promote world community. To achieve this goal, however, they must abandon their absolutist religious claims, according to Talmon. Rather they must recognize that their universalism is eschatological. Hence they must resist any desire to realize it pre-eschatologically through active proselytization.[16]

On the Christian side the argument would run along the lines that it must always be expressed within the love context central to Jesus' own ministry. All forms of hatred or persecution of Jews are outlawed by the New Testament love ethic. Many in this school would also point to Romans 9—11 as a basis for a new theology of Judaism. The Christian universalistic claim is unquestionable in their eyes, though the continued existence of the Jewish community remains a "mystery" that must be respected by Christians. Associated with this line of thinking would be names such as Kurt Hruby, Jacques Maritain, Jean Daniélou and Augustin Cardinal Bea.[17]

In more poetic form, both the Jews and Christians who advocate this approach would in effect be saying the following: Let us wait for the advent of the Messiah. Then we can ask him whether this is his first or his second coming.

While I respect the view of these Jewish and Christian scholars, my experience in the dialogue forces me to take up another option. The enrichment and insight I have received from living contact with Jews and Judaism has given me new religious meaning and in many ways enhanced and deepened my understanding of the Incarnation. But it has also forced upon me a profound re-evaluation of traditional claims of Christian superiority and universality. I am not the same Christian person I was before my involvement in the dialogue. Hence the need to restate Christological meanings in the light of this experience which I know has also been shared by other Christian men and women involved in the dialogue.

I include this very personal statement lest the subsequent chapters be interpreted as merely an attempt to be theologically innovative. Theology is experienced meaning seeking expression in a faith setting. In the categories put forth by Schreiter, my experience in the dialogue has overcome elements of non-meaning in my previous articulation of Christian faith. As a result, a reformulated expression of that faith is impossible to avoid. I hope that those who may not agree with the Christological reformulation offered in the following pages will at least appreciate its basis in a deep, dialogic faith experience.

2
Christology and the Christian-Jewish Encounter

In the years since Vatican Council II, there has emerged a steadily growing core of Christian theologians with a deep involvement in the dialogue with Jews. These scholars have begun to take a hard look at the traditional ways in which the Church has expressed the significance of the Christ event vis-à-vis Judaism. Though some began their work prior to the Council, the new interest in the Jewish-Christian relationship generated by the Vatican Council's *Declaration on the Relationship of the Church to Non-Christian Religions* has given new prominence to their work.

These scholars can basically be categorized into two groupings. The first has tended to view the Christ event as the extension of the one basic covenant, originally made with the Jewish people and still in their possession, to the non-Jewish world. The second school prefers to look at Judaism and Christianity as two distinct covenantal religions that are different but complementary in an ultimate sense. The labels single-covenant school and double-covenant school have become standard ways of differentiating them. But, as it shall become clear later on in this chapter, there are no simple terms that do full justice to the theological positions which have been developing. In addition, a number of the major figures in the dialogue appear to have shifted their perspective in recent years.

Beneath the often significant differences between these two basic theological approaches stands a common conviction that the assertion by traditional Christian faith that the coming of the Church through the Christ event brought to fulfillment all that was of any value in Judaism must be seriously challenged. These theologians have come to recognize

8

that Christians need to view the Jewish "no" to Jesus as a positive contribution to the ultimate salvation of humankind, not merely an act of unfaithfulness or haughty blindness. But they are also aware of deep-seated problems involved in any attempt at modifying classical Christian claims. For in taking up the theological dimensions of the relationship between the Church and the Synagogue we are touching upon a central nerve in Christianity. Its basic self-definition is at stake. There will be need to deal forthrightly with credal statements couched in a vocabulary of the "new Moses," the "new covenant," "the new Israel," and the "new Jerusalem" that has been central to Christian theology from the very beginning days of the Church.

Both schools of thought go well beyond the initial explorations of the Christian-Jewish relationships, undertaken by an earlier generation of Christian theologians such as Charles Journet,[18] Jean Daniélou,[19] Hans Urs von Balthasar[20] and Augustin Cardinal Bea[21] who remain uncompromising on the centrality of Christ and the fulfillment that his coming brought, but who still found ways to leave some theological space for Judaism, often by building on the "mystery" theology offered by St. Paul in Romans 9—11. Some comentators have referred to these earlier attempts as "theologies of discontinuity" over against the more recent "theologies of continuity" whether the latter be of the single or double covenant variety.[22]

Single-Covenant Perspectives

Turning first to the single covenant approach we find the writings of Monika Hellwig. While she has never presented a fully developed Christology reflective of her experience in the dialogue, Hellwig has given some indications of the directions she feels such a Christology would need to take.[23] For her the simultaneous and complementary participation of Christianity and Judaism in the same covenant requires a restatement of several theological concepts central to the faith expression of the Church for centuries. The most crucial of these is the traditional Christian assertion that the long-awaited Messiah came in the person of Jesus of Nazareth. Those who recognized him were welcomed into his kingdom, whether they be Jews or Gentiles. Among his own people, however, the majority refused to accept him with the consequent punishment of being left in outer darkness. Such an approach to Christ, she strongly insists, represents a tragic oversimplification of what in fact the original apostolic community claimed for the Christ event. A more accurate formulation would be that the cry of the early Christian community, "Jesus is Lord and Christ," was and remains

> . . . a prophetic assertion by which Christians have pledged themselves to a task of salvation yet to be accomplished. Even to the Christian there is a most important sense in which Jesus is not yet Messiah. The eschatological tension has not been resolved. What may be expected in the Messianic fulfillment has not yet become manifest in the world— that there shall be peace among men; that the weak shall have no cause to fear the strong; that a spirit of healing and joy shall be all pervasive. Logically the Messianic Event should be seen as lengthy, complex, unfinished and mysterious.[24]

Hellwig is well aware that some may feel her line of reasoning evades what many would regard as the fundamental point of cleavage between Jews and Christians, namely, that the Church recognized Jesus as divine and understood the inner life of God as triune while Jews reject both claims as blasphemous. While there is no simple way around this seemingly insuperable obstacle, she is convinced that the contemporary Christian discussions about the nature of religious language do give us some hope that a new perspective may be developed. As a result of these discussions we are beginning to understand more clearly the analogical nature of the term "person" when used in reference to God, and that fifth-century Christological definitions of one person and two natures were no more than "a cautious naming of the unknown in Christian experience of divine intervention."[25]

We need therefore to change our attitude toward the statements "Jesus is Son of God" and "Jesus is divine" from simple equation to interpretation where exact meaning continues to remain quite elusive. The Christ event must now be expressed primarily in phenomenological terms. Jesus is the place of encounter of the human person with the transcendent God, something Christians have experienced as central in all human existence. Such an interpretation becomes even more significant, according to Hellwig, in the context of the Jewish prohibition against idols which proscribes against the making of divine images, out of the deep conviction that there exists only one image of God that reveals anything of importance, namely, the human person.

Several foci are apparent in Hellwig's approach. In the first place, she joins in the protest against those Christians who would easily describe Jesus as the expected Jewish Messiah. Her reason for rejecting this interpretation seems ultimately rooted in the experience of the human community within history: the promised characteristics of the Messianic kingdom simply are not to be seen in our midst.

It is important to highlight this point. For as we move through a representative sample of theologians coming out of the contemporary Christian-Jewish dialogue, the experience of history will clearly emerge as one of the principal counter-claims against the traditional Christian assertion about the arrival of the Messianic age in Jesus. Clearly articulated or not, these theologians are working out of a methodology which allows for historical experience within the Church to serve as a basis for theological reformulation.

On the positive side Hellwig appears to center the meaning of the Christ event around the notion of the Incarnation rather than the fulfillment of Messianic promises relative to history and the kingdom. I consider this a step in the right direction. She does not really delve into the unique features of Incarnational theology nor ask whether it constitutes a central component of every adequate understanding of human salvation. Neither does she state with any great clarity what revelational role Judaism continues to play in the post-Christ event period. The interdependence and separation of Christians and Jews within a single covenantal tradition is never explained in a comprehensive manner in her present writings.

She appears to view the two faith traditions as complementary aspects of the same fundamental eschatological reality. And that eschatological reality must be seen as future, by Christians as well as by Jews. Messiahship constitutes a mission incumbent upon the entire Church of God (i.e., Christians and Jews) to realize in history. The one, continuous covenant can be described as new after the Christ event only in the sense that now it embraces both Jews and Gentiles. Jesus has allowed non-Jews to enter the election, first bestowed upon the people of Israel. Hence Christians must look to God's continuing revelation in contemporary Jewish experience to see what God is saying of himself. By implication, though Hellwig does not state this clearly, the revelation of God within the experience of the Church likewise becomes a barometer for Jewish faith expression. From what she has given us thus far one would have to include her among the Christian theologians who basically see Christianity as Judaism for the Gentiles. For me this ultimately remains an unsatisfactory articulation of the relationship. However, on some occasions Hellwig hints that she may want to go further, especially in terms of the Incarnation.

Another theologian who can best be classified within the single covenant school is Paul Van Buren. His involvement in the dialogue has been of somewhat recent origin, but it has profoundly affected his theological outlook.

His first attempt to express this change in theological perspective came in his small volume *The Burden of Freedom*.[26] This work largely consists of a frontal, uncompromising denunciation of traditional Christian interpretations of Jesus' relationship to Judaism. He is especially strong in his critique of the so-called "Judaeo-Christian tradition" which has been so popular in Christian circles in this century. In this attack Van Buren joins company with several leading Jewish scholars such as Arthur Cohen and Hans Jonas.[27]

As Van Buren interprets the data at hand, Western Christianity has basically stamped out any authentic Jewish components in favor of a pagan-Christian tradition. Auschwitz for him represents the ultimate poverty of this Christian paganism.

So the first step for the contemporary Church is to rejoin Judaism. Theologically this will not prove an easy undertaking for the Church because of what Van Buren terms a tremendous cover-up which began before Christianity was even a hundred years old. This cover-up was basically a response to the realization that the characteristics of the Messianic age were nowhere to be seen. Rather than alter its theology the Church pushed the realization of the Messianic age to a non-historical, "higher" realm. With this shift completed, the way was opened to proclaim the Easter event as a triumph in every respect:

> What it had not accomplished, including such minor details as the end of human suffering, sickness, injustice, oppression and torture, death, much of it horrible, of men, women, and children, not omitting those slaughtered by the Romans, in Jerusalem in the year 70—all such details were simply scaled down in value in the mythological scenario as being of only transient concern. After all, with eternal life won, why care about actual human life?. . . The more triumphalistic the mythological interpretation of Easter, the more Christianity could calmly ignore the world which it had claimed that God so loved.[28]

It is imperative, according to Van Buren, for the Church to go back and listen to the original apostolic testimony regarding Jesus. In this respect Van Buren's call is similar to that of Monika Hellwig. Both feel that later Christian theology has obscured and distorted the initial (and in their view authentic) understanding of the Christ event.

In a multi-volume work, Van Buren is currently in the process of further refining the ideas he launched in *The Burden of Freedom*. Thus far, with the appearance of the first volume,[29] he has provided only a glimpse of the directions he plans to follow. Van Buren now insists that the Church has an identity apart from Judaism, a divinely appointed identity. It is not merely one among several Jewish sects. Israel has two fundamental branches, Judaism and Christianity. Both are essential. The Church is the community of the Gentiles who have been drawn by the God of the Jews to worship him and make his love known among the nations. Christianity's developing appreciation of Judaism in no way implies a dilution of its affirmation of Jesus as the Christ. Nor must the Church stop confessing Jesus as Son of God. Van Buren believes that the German New Testament scholar Martin Hengel has convincingly demonstrated in his volume *The Son of Man*[30] that this title has profoundly Jewish roots.

According to Van Buren, the new revelation in Jesus was the manifestation of the divine will that Gentiles too are welcome to walk in God's way. For those Gentiles who through the Christ event came for the first time to be drawn into the plan of God, what took place in Jesus could not be understood as merely one episode in the history of salvation. Rather it "marked a genuinely new beginning, a step out and beyond the circles of God's eternal covenant with His people, the Jews. But it surely cannot and does not detract from, much less annul, that covenant."[31]

As Van Buren sees it, it is legitimate, even necessary, for Christians to refer to Jesus as the Christ. But he is not the Jewish Messiah as traditionally claimed by Christians. In some ways Van Buren might be better placed in the double-covenant school since he insists that the revelation of the plan of God to Gentiles through the ministry and person of Jesus is somehow different from the vision accorded the Jewish people. Nonetheless, it is best to identify him with the single-covenant position in view of his great stress that Israel, that God's way, is ultimately one. The extension of the Messianic vision to the Gentiles was already implied, according to Van Buren, in the covenant with the Jews, "for Israel has always worshipped the God of Israel as the King of the universe."[32] Van Buren, then, appears to maintain that Judaism and Christianity are both valid and complementary glimpses into the same life and love of the Creator God.

Van Buren's approach shows promise in several respects. It rejects the unfounded Christian contention that Jesus completely fulfilled Jewish messianic expectations; it emphasizes that the experience of history in part forces upon the Church a reformulation of its attitude toward Jesus' relationship with Judaism; it highlights the universality implied in the principal covenant with Israel; while it maintains a difference between the perceptions of God's plan for humanity enjoyed by Jews and Christians respectively, it nonetheless posits their seeming equality and ultimate compatibility.

The biggest drawback to the Van Buren thesis, at least as stated thus far, is that it says nothing about the nature of the difference between the Jewish version of the one covenant and its Christian expression. Van Buren says that the same plan of God came to Moses, to the prophets and finally in the flesh and blood of the man Jesus of Nazareth. Contrary to many scholars, Van Buren does not seem to stress any fundamental development or change in the perception of this plan even during its exclusively Jewish phase. Did the granting of the vision to the Gentiles through Jesus add anything to the vision? Was it different only because it was with the Gentiles? Where does this leave Jewish Christians? And why start a new community called the Church when Gentiles were already entering the Jewish community in some numbers at the time of Jesus? Van Buren also seems to go against some significant contemporary Jewish scholarship on Jesus, indicating ways in which his teaching went beyond even the most progressive forms of Judaism in the period.

Up till now, my judgment would have to be that Van Buren's approach leaves little rationale for the continued existence of Christianity as an independent religion and that it undercuts any claim that Christianity constitutes a major world religious tradition in its own right. He relates the Christological experience in a way that parallels the outlook of Rosemary Ruether, which we shall examine shortly. In this sense he is more radical than Hellwig who appears to leave room for unique features in the Incarnational aspects of Christology.

Perhaps Van Buren's thesis will undergo significant modification in its future, more developed form. I am convinced that any Christology which fails to provide for some unique, central role for Christ in the history of salvation barters away too much of the Christian covenant and stands little chance of acceptance by the Church at large. Saying this, however, does not imply that the Christological vision of human salvation is automatically superior to the Jewish vision (or other religious visions) or that Judaism does not likewise have a central role which complements that of Christianity.

A third example of a single-covenant theology can be found in the work of A. Roy Eckardt. A word of caution must be posed, however, regarding this classification, for, as we shall see, Eckardt has made some substantial modifications in his point of view.

Over the years Eckardt, one of the most prolific contributors to theological thought in the Jewish-Christian dialogue, has steadfastly clung to the position that Christianity has not replaced Israel in the drama of human salvation and that Israel's divinely determined vocation continues intact into our time. God's design, according to Eckardt, preordained that a majority of the people of Israel would say "no" to the Christ event. Eckardt sees Israel and the Church standing in dialectical tension to each other within the one covenant. At least this has been his long-standing thesis. Each carries a different function in salvation history and each is prone to a corresponding temptation. Israel's primary role remains to turn inward to the Jewish people while Christianity is outer-directed toward the Gentiles. The corresponding temptations are that the Jews may allow their election to produce self-exaltation. The Church's reliance on grace as given, on the other hand, may lead to a false sense of freedom from all duties prescribed by the Torah. Put another way, in standing firm against any false dichotomy between the sacred and the secular, Israel may unintentionally oversecularize the kingdom of God. Meanwhile in entering the secular world Christianity may experience the temptation to overspiritualize the kingdom of God and negate the fundamental goodness inherent in God's creation. As Eckardt sees it:

> Jesus of Nazareth, called the Christ, embodies the paradox of uniting Jews with Christians and of separating Jews from Christians. There is simply no way around or beyond this stern fact. Any discussion of the Jewish-Christian relationship must presuppose both elements in this ultimate tension. The mystery of Israel's election has found a continuation and fulfillment in the mystery of the Incarnation of God in Jesus Christ.[33]

For Eckardt the revelation in Jesus Christ, though unique in some respects, is in principle no more significant than the divine action through which the Jewish people secured their vocation. The Christian proclamation of the Christ event can depict the Church as successor to Israel in one respect alone. In virtue of the ministry of Jesus the wall that had previously divided Jews and Gentiles has been permanently shattered. The coming of Jesus unlocked the abiding covenant with the people Israel for entrance by the nations of the world in a fashion that Judaism has never quite imagined possible.

More recent theological reflection by Eckardt finds him expressing some hesitation about his previous single-covenant thesis. He feels that it is now time for the Christian community to allow Israel to move in whatever direction she judges best for herself, even if this should involve severing covenantal ties with Christianity. Eckardt makes it clear that his staunch defense of the single-covenant position in the past was predicated on his deep concern about Christian supersessionist approaches to Judaism. If and when Christianity succeeds, however, in overcoming the perverse desire to bill itself as the replacement for "old Israel," then it may be perfectly legitimate for the two faith communities to go their separate ways while maintaining a relationship of mutual love and respect. He writes:

> I think that my earlier and repeated insistence upon the membership of Christians in the Jewish family has been determined in considerable measure by the necessary warfare against Christian supersessionism, the fantasy that the "New Israel" has replaced original Israel. Suppose that this fantasy is at last overcome. Must the family stay together? I am uncertain how to answer. I do know that loved ones part from one another and go their different ways—though they need not thereby cease their loving or their caring. Indeed it may be that parting must take place by the very decree of love and for the sake of love.[34]

As Eckardt has further developed his thought, especially as a consequence of his research on the Nazi Holocaust, he has become more inclined to say that many of the theological categories such as "covenant" that are commonplace in traditional descriptions of the Jewish-Christian relationship have lost their former validity. Judaism and Christianity both must be rethought as a result of the shattering reality represented by the Holocaust. In studies prepared for an ongoing association of Christian scholars called the Israel Study Group, Eckardt has suggested among other things that perhaps we should no longer call the Jews a covenantal people in the traditional sense of the term. He likewise asks whether the Christian doctrine of the Resurrection need not be dropped from the Creed if the Church is ever to finally rid itself of its classical distortion of Judaism. Auschwitz has for him undercut the centuries-long belief in God's faithfulness to Israel. The old interpretation of the covenant was "consumed once and for all in the flames of the crematoria, its breath was snuffed out forever in the gas chambers."[35]

After Auschwitz only one type of covenant can be discussed relative to the Jewish people. It is a covenant of the divine agony which places them in a state of unqualified ordinariness, of unmitigated secularity within this world.

For the Church Auschwitz has put an end to the belief in the

Resurrection of Jesus. It is not that the Nazi Holocaust has eradicated this traditional claim in Eckardt's eyes. Rather Auschwitz finally and decisively showed the basic error of that belief in the first place. For Christians today who are serious about putting an end to the degraded theological position in which the Church has held Judaism, resurrection can have only a future connotation. Eckardt rejects all contemporary theological attempts to interpret the Resurrection in a symbolic rather than a literal sense. In Eckardt's words:

> That Jewish man from the Galilee sleeps now. He sleeps with the other Jewish dead, with all the disconsolate and the scattered ones of the murder camps, and with the unnumbered dead of the human and non-human family. But Jesus of Nazareth shall be raised. So too shall the small Hungarian children who were bured alive at Auschwitz.[36]

With respect to Jesus, therefore, Resurrection remains an exclusively futuristic category. This future resurrection of Jesus will carry special meaning for Christians because it is his history through which the Gentiles were brought into the covenant with Israel. In a parallel fashion the future resurrection of Abraham and Moses will carry distinctive significance for the eschatological community of Jews.

His most recent statements seem to place Eckardt back within the single-covenant school of thought despite his somewhat radical reinterpretation of the covenantal tradition. It is not totally clear where precisely he stands at this moment regarding the reservations about a single covenant which he advanced in 1974. Without doubt his thinking on the matter remains fluid.

Eckardt's approach shows some of the same strengths and weaknesses displayed by the Van Buren thesis. They touch each other in many areas, though the differences between them should not be overlooked. Eckardt joins Van Buren in seeing Christianity as essentially Judaism for the Gentiles, though he insists that the coming of Christ exploded Jewish conceptions in ways that Judaism was unprepared to accept. Eckardt, like Van Buren, seems to fall into a basically static view of the meaning of the *Way* that the Sinai experience made known to Jews and the Christ event revealed to Christians. Some comments of Eckardt's do suggest nonetheless that the universalization of the covenant in Jesus did constitute a kind of qualitative development. The criticisms with respect to the content of the Christian Gospel made of Van Buren need to be repeated in analyzing Eckardt. If the only difference between the Messianic vision of Christianity and Judaism respectively is that the Gentiles now understand the plan of human salvation, then why bother with a separate faith community? Why not simply reincorporate the Church into the Synagogue, at least on the level of theological theory?

Eckardt's insistence on the theological significance of Auschwitz is a point well made, though I do not feel it rules out maintenance of the category of resurrection as he argues it must. Christianity past or present does not rise or fall on a literal interpretation of the Resurrection. Taking the Resurrection as a symbolic category does not mean that there is no reality involved in the notion. Resurrection can be reconciled both with the Auschwitz experience and a reformulated Christology that leaves theological space and meaning for Judaism. I will return to this point later on in this volume. For the moment, it is sufficient to note that for me the Resurrection does not stand as the basic Christological affirmation but rather as a corollary of the notion of the Incarnation. Stating the relationship in this fashion guards against that false, though frequent, Christian triumphalism stemming from the doctrine of the Resurrection which Eckardt has rightly condemned.

The final representative of the single-covenant school that we shall examine is J. Coos Schoneveld. As a Christian deeply involved for many years in the dialogue in Israel with the Ecumenical Theological Research Fraternity, Schoneveld brings a perspective to the Christological question rooted in a living encounter with Jewish life in Israel.[37]

Schoneveld's views have been very much conditioned by the thinking of Paul Van Buren relative to the Jewish-Christian relationship. He clearly acknowledges this debt. Schoneveld joins Van Buren and Eckardt in the position that through Jesus the Gentiles were accorded a vision of the plan for human salvation given to the Jewish people through Abraham and Moses. Jesus has enabled Christians to worship the God of Israel and to become his sons and daughters. Schoneveld goes beyond even Van Buren and Eckardt in rejecting any fundamental newness in the Christ event. While Van Buren and Eckardt retain a certain ambiguity on the matter, Schoneveld makes his position quite clear:

> When we look at the Church's life and teaching, has anything been added to the Torah? I have searched for a long time for anything new. In fact nothing new is there, which goes beyond a certain change of emphasis or a certain different nuance in comparison with Jewish teachings of the first century, except that through Jesus the Gentiles have been admitted and the range of the teaching of the Torah has

become much wider. What is given in the Torah comes to us Gentiles through Jesus Christ.[38]

For Schoneveld it is illegitimate for Christians to call Jesus the Messiah. His coming has not brought about the realities of the Messianic Kingdom, and for Christians to totally redefine the term is hardly a responsible use of language. Christians may properly refer to Jesus only as "Christ" (which even in the early Church quickly shed its Messianic implications), "Lord," "Savior," or some similar doxological term.

There is definitely only one covenant. Schoneveld does not exhibit even the least bit of hesitation on this score. Christians have received certain dispensations from the commandments that were given to Israel. Christians share in the promises originally made to Israel and show their faithfulness to these promises in ways other than those developed by the Jewish community. In some ways there is a greater flexibility possible in the Christian response, but it is not superior to the Jewish one nor is it based on some substantially new insight into the salvific plan of God. Schoneveld's strong, unhesitating rejection of any Messianic explanation of the Christ event adds weight to the absolute necessity of such a rejection as can come up with nothing new or unique in the teachings of Jesus in comparison with Judaism of his period is open to serious question. But Schoneveld's strong, unhesitating rejection of any Messianic explanation of the Christ event adds weight to the absolute necessity of such a rejection as the first major step in Christological reformulation. It is becoming increasingly clear that nearly every Christian scholar, regardless of how he or she would move in creating a new Christology, has concluded from a serious investigation of the Judaism of Jesus' time that traditional claims for his Messiahship must be dropped as unwarranted on the basis of the data at hand.

Double-Covenant Perspectives

One of the first Christian scholars to probe not only the roots of classical antisemitism in the churches but also to reflect on the theological dimensions of the Christian-Jewish relationship has been the Anglican scholar James Parkes. His many writings broke new ground in the thought patterns of Christianity relative to Judaism.

Parkes anchors his version of the "double-covenant" theory in what he calls the different but complementary revelation of "Sinai" and "Calvary." These two terms summarize the quintessence of each community's basic faith experience. Parkes interprets the "Sinai" experience as basically communal in orientation while "Calvary" revolves much more around an understanding of the individual person. He writes:

> That highest purpose of God which Sinai reveals to men as community, Calvary reveals to man as an end in himself. The difference between the two events, both of which from the metaphysical standpoint are identical as expressions of the infinite in the finite, of the eternal in the world of space and time, lies in the fact that the first could not be fulfilled by a brief demonstration of a divine community in action; but the second could not be fulfilled except by a life lived under human conditions from birth to death.[39]

Parkes claims that a stress on the person as individual began to grow in Jewish literature in the exilic and post-exilic periods. Witness, he says, the concern with the individual in Jeremiah, Ezekiel, the Wisdom literature, Job and among the Pharisees. It is out of this movement that Jesus stepped into history. The revelation represented by Calvary did not replace Sinai. On the other hand, Sinai could not simply absorb it and remain unchanged. In the life and teaching of Jesus the earlier revelation and the new revelation co-exist in creative tension. In the Christian concern with the individual as person, nothing is taken away from the power or importance of the working out in history of the revelation of Sinai.

Parkes makes it clear that Sinai did not mark the beginning of human concern with the moral problem of people in society. Before Sinai were centuries of experience which were both human discoveries and divine revelations. What occurred at Sinai was the full development of a long, gradual growth in the human person's understanding of community. It took centuries to realize the full extent of Sinai, and even today the complete meaning of that revelation remains elusive. In the same manner, what had been growing in Judaism since the period of the exile attained its full development with Calvary. It has been subject to interpretation ever since:

> The divine plan for human society is given its full meaning when the divine plan for man as person is revealed within it. In Jesus the ultimate unity is not destroyed; Paul still struggles to maintain it. But in the complex setting of first century life the two halves broke apart, and the beginning of the second century witnessed the religions confronting each other—Judaism and Christianity.[40]

For Parkes, Judaism and Christianity are inextricably linked together as equals. The tension that exists between them is not rooted in some metaphysic forced upon history from without, but in the perennial and inevitable experience of tension in ordinary human life between the human person as social being and as individual, as an ultimate value in himself or herself, as one formed in the likeness of God. This tension extends to the whole of life and will endure until the end of days.

Parkes has expressed serious misgivings about what he regards as an overly Christocentric orientation in much of Christian theology. The writings of his later years try to respond to this unfortunate orientation by offering a new understanding of the Trinity. Seeing this doctrine as a possible opening for improving Jewish-Christian understanding rather than an obstacle to such advancement is unique to Parkes. For most theologians in the dialogue the Trinity represents a doctrinal position that separates Jews from Christians rather than a model for a new proximity.

Parkes is convinced, however, that the Trinity is a very basic tool for looking upon Church and Synagogue theologically as possessing complementary rather than mutually exclusive and antagonistic roles in the plan of human salvation. Rather than emphasizing "person" in the Trinity he highlights what he calls three "channels" whereby divine power reaches creation. Each of these "channels," though different in orientation and emphasis, is of equal value. Thus, for him, correct relations between Judaism and Christianity consist in a creative tension within a unified trinitarian theology. The complementary roles enjoyed by Judaism and Christianity make their respective missions complementary as well. Israel bears witness to the reality of an elected community while the Church testifies to the covenantal relationship with each individual person.

Parkes' analysis of trends within later Judaism and how they affected the ministry and teaching of Jesus will contribute some definitely positive elements to a reformulated Christology. His emphasis on development within Judaism and how this led its people to components of the message preached by Jesus is most important. His model has begun to allow theological room for both Judaism and Christianity, though his trinitarian model for doing so will likely not be judged a useful tool in the final analysis. He has also addressed more directly and effectively the content question relative to the Christ event than some of the other theologians in the dialogue. Emphasizing the Christian Gospel as having to do primarily with the salvific dimension of individual existence is definitely on the right track, though he overdraws it somewhat.

The most serious lack in Parkes' approach is his failure to connect his "individual" model for Christianity with the Incarnation and to probe more deeply the Judaism of Jesus' day. There remains a degree of superficiality about his position relative to New Testament development. Still, his studies constitute an important breakthrough, one that can serve as a genuine point of departure for rethinking the issue of Jesus and Judaism.[41]

Parkes, despite opting for the double-covenant approach, considers it essential for Christians to study Second Temple Judaism in depth if they are to properly interpret the New Testament message. This is a point that needs to be underlined with respect to all the double-covenant theologians. While each wishes to maintain a distinctive revelatory role for both Sinai and the Christ event, this in no way is meant to diminish their conviction that the New Testament cannot be properly exegeted apart from an understanding of its Jewish context.

Another Christian with long-standing credentials in the dialogue is the biblical scholar J. Coert Rylaarsdam. After years of reflection on the theological relationship between Judaism and Christianity, Rylaarsdam has concluded that the conflict between the two faith-communities cannot be properly explained unless we are sensitive to the presence of two distinctive covenants within the Jewish biblical tradition.

The first of these, the covenant with Israel, had its feet firmly implanted in the flow of history, laying stress on a socio-religious union called into being by God. Central to its conception was a mutual pact of faithfulness and responsibility negotiated between God and the chosen people. It is characterized by the continuity between Gospel and Law and includes both the theme of covenantal recital and the theme of obligation. These themes are reflective of a belief that the only truly meaningful reality is the world of people and history, especially as witnessed in the particularity of the Israel specially chosen by Yahweh. This covenant looks to the future. It relates a salvation history replete with interventions by God in behalf of his people. History, in the perspective of this covenant, remains an open-ended process. Since its basic élan was not easily compatible with interpretations given the Christ event, it tended to receive short shrift from the authors of the New Testament.

The second covenant highlighted by Rylaarsdam placed its focus on the person of David. As he interprets it, this covenant embodied a decidedly eschatological cast. Its principal characteristic is the holiness connected with Mount Zion and the divine presence as revealed through the Davidic dynasty. The appearance of this covenantal tradition marked a new beginning in Judaism. There was a tension evident with the earlier covenant.

This was finally moderated by a measure of accommodation with it while avoiding total absorption. The Davidic covenant looked to and celebrated a supra-temporal order of meaning. God is depicted as king of creation and of the nation. The earlier covenant's stress on law and history is largely absent from the second. Whereas one finds no Alpha-Omega dimensions in the future-oriented first covenant, the second celebrates Alpha with a concentration on its significance for the present time.

Rylaarsdam believes that the continual tension between these two covenants was responsible for the growth of several sectarian religious groups. One of these was the eschatologically oriented Christian Church. This new faith community was beset by the same tensions found in biblical Judaism but the priority of the two covenants had been reversed. Rylaarsdam puts it this way:

> However Jesus may have understood his vocation, at the outset Christians interpreted his career as an eschatological event. He had overcome the world (*olam*), relativized history—or even abolished it. Except for some sectarian movements, Judaism thought more historically than eschatologically. It awaited the transformation and redemption of the world. So the Jews said that the Messiah had not come. But the Gentiles believed. And the Christians wrote a commentary on the Hebrew Bible and called it the New Testament. Its accent is overwhelmingly eschatological. Therefore it has now become the primary occasion for the dilemmas of Christology.[42]

The Christians who wrote the New Testament were a Jewish sect. This, Rylaarsdam insists, must never be forgotten. They were sectarians because of the one-sided position they took relative to the interaction of the two covenants. For a moment they lost sight of the paradoxical nature of the relationship within Judaism. They tried to reduce the full meaning of human history to the eschatological perception of the Davidic covenant, but time soon showed them the error of their ways. Nineteen centuries of Christian history can be read, according to Rylaarsdam, as a progressive attempt to overcome this initial mistake. Retention of the Hebrew Scriptures as revelation has assisted the Church in this task, for it insured that the link with its Jewish roots has never been totally lost by Christianity.

Rylaarsdam thus posits the existence of two biblical covenants. They are not the two successive covenants usually called old and new testaments by Christians. Rather the two authentic covenantal traditions run through both the Hebrew Scriptures and the New Testament. With this perspective the understanding of the relationship between Judaism and Christianity must be radically reshaped from its traditional mold. If both Judaism and Christianity continue to revolve around the same two covenants that are paradoxically related to one another, then the Church-Synagogue relationship, whatever its concrete tensions at a given moment, must be viewed theologically as one of mutual interdependence.

Rylaarsdam's attempt to articulate a new theological model for the Jewish-Christian relationship shows some promising features. It underscores the complementary nature of the two covenantal traditions. It also tries to give legitimate, distinctive theological space to each. There is a certain measure of truth in the explanations of the two covenants as focusing on history (Judaism) and on the Davidic line (Christianity) respectively. But Rylaarsdam has not related his position sufficiently well to the growth in Jewish consciousness taking place during the Second Temple period. His outlook on the two covenants is too static. He also fails to deal adequately with the Incarnational dimension of Christianity, focusing too much on the Messianic.

Again, as with some of the other scholars we have been examining, the fundamental directions Rylaarsdam takes are perhaps more significant than the precise model he offers. The model in its present form will simply not stand up to full scholarly scrutiny. It needs major revamping, although some important, indispensable building blocks are present.

A third exponent of a double-covenant approach is Gregory Baum. Though involved in the effort to eradicate antisemitism for many years, he has formally addressed the theological dimensions of the Jewish-Christian relationship only in recent years.

Baum has not evolved a thorough theological statement on the meaning of the Christ event in the light of Judaism.[43] He does insist, however, that Judaism's destiny is not merely to disappear after the Christ event. Judaism continues to exercise a positive impact on the fulfillment of the divine plan of salvation. The saving presence of God remains alive in the post-Easter Jewish community. A reformulated Christology that takes Judaism seriously, as Baum insists must be the case, needs to abandon any claim that Jesus is the one mediator without whom salvation is impossible to find. He has great difficulty with attempts to solve this problem by categorizing Jews and other religious peoples as "anonymous Christians," as Karl Rahner does. It appears that Baum continues to maintain a universal significance for the Christ event. There is, however, some doubt about this. In his Introduction to the Ruether volume, he both endorses her basic approach which seems to rule out any universal significance and yet continues to speak of an absolute and all-embracing dimension to the revelation in Christ. He does assert, however, that whatever universality is attributable to the Christ event cannot be interpreted as invalidating the significance of other religions. What it does is to offer a critique applicable to all religions, Christianity included. What occurred in the Christ event was the realization that God's full victory is assured, though not presently realized. Therefore, any Messianic claims relative to Jesus must be spoken in the future tense, not as present-day reality.

Jesus will become the Christ, in Baum's view, only at the end of days. Christians witness to a divine reality that can be discovered by all peoples, even though articulation of this discovery may utilize different symbols and language as we move from one culture to another. The following statement by Baum brings together well these various components in his Christological outline:

> What is this Christian witness with universal relevance? ... I propose that the Church's witness with universal meaning and power is the message of God's approaching kingdom. Jesus Christ is the unique instrument and servant of this kingdom, and through his humiliation and glory we have been assured of God's ultimate victory over evil, already pressing in upon us now.... What is upon us, in whatever religion or whatever culture, is the divine judgment revealing the ideological deformation of truth, the power games, the structures of domination, the institutional pathologies, the workings of sin that oppose life in its fullness. What is equally upon us is God's life-giving grace, which enables us as persons and as peoples to sever ourselves from a destructive past and move creatively into the future. This judgment and this grace are offered wherever people are; and the Christian witness, offered to them in word and action, facilitates the discernment of the divine language. The Church's eschatological witness constitutes its universal vocation.[44]

The strength of Baum's position lies in its sense of development in revelatory consciousness, in its attempt to sketch out a Christology that does not invalidate Judaism, and in its emphasis in this Christological sketch on a significance for the Christ event that could be tied to themes of Second Temple Judaism and of Incarnational theology. The most striking drawback is Baum's failure to provide any description of the content of the ongoing Jewish covenant. Stating the continuing validity of this covenant is certainly a step forward. But without explicating in some way its core elements, there is the possibility in Baum's current position, as Michael McGarry well notes,[45] that Christians might be doing nothing more than pushing the traditional notion of Judaism's invalidation by the Christ event one step back to the end of time. If this were the case, then Baum's position could not be classified as thoroughly positive in its appreciation of Judaism.

No doubt the most radical attempt to address the question of Christology and Judaism has come from Rosemary Ruether. Her writings convey a deep conviction that any ultimate and permanent resolution of the centuries of Christian hostility toward Jews and Judaism is totally dependent on the creation of a new Christology. The roots of Christian antisemitism reach back into the Christologies fashioned by the New Testament writers and "perfected" by the Church Fathers.

Ruether joins the other dialogue theologians in rejecting any contention that the Messianic age came to pass in the Christ event. History will not allow us to escape from such a rejection. Christians have been seriously remiss in not realizing this up till now. For her, human history remains every bit as much, perhaps even more, mired in ambiguity, sickness, sin and death, as was the case prior to the coming of Jesus. If the Church persists in affirming that the term "Christ" signifies the Messiah of Israel's hope, then it must likewise appreciate that

> . . . from the standpoint of that faith of Israel itself, there is no possibility of talking about the Messiah having come (much less of having come two thousand years ago, with all the evil history that has reigned from that time until this) when the reign of God has not come.[46]

She unqualifiedly affirms that "what Christianity has in Jesus is not the Messiah, but a Jew who hoped for the kingdom of God and who died in that hope."[47]

The Jewish tradition, Ruether maintains, cannot separate the coming of the Messiah and the appearance of the Messianic age. The two are simultaneous—in actuality, one and the same event. Judaism has generally placed its stress primarily on the Messianic age rather than on a Messianic figure. The problem is that Christianity took up this traditional Jewish belief in the Messianic age of the future and "imported" it into current history. The Church declared that evil was conquered once and for all by the Christ event. This resulted in a false solution to the ultimate crisis of all human existence, the crisis that divided the historical from the eschatological. The entire span of human history prior to the Christ event could be regarded in this perspective as the period of unredeemed humanity. All those who reject the Christian revelation, especially Jews, maintain their residence in this era. Christian faith, however, allows men and women to pass into the new historical period of Messianic glory. Instead of illuminating the inevitable tension between the historical and the eschatological, Christian Messianism helped to fashion a false consciousness "allowing the Church to dress historical ambiguities in the dress of finality and absolute truth. This new historical era and people are seen as standing not merely in a relative but in an absolute supersessionary relationship to Judaism and to all human possibilities 'before.' "[48] Ruether terms this process the illegitimate "historicizing of the eschatological." It is a central idea in her writings on the Jewish-Christian relationship.

Ruether sees absolutely no validity for a Messianic notion in Christianity unless that notion is related to an ultimate, future event which will abolish all suffering and injustice on this earth. Granting absolute finality to the expectations which arose as a consequence of Jesus' ministry and death represents for Ruether a flawed way, one might say a fatal flaw, of understanding the Church's eschatological dimension. This false appropriation of eschatological meaning on the part of Christians has led to disastrous results for Jews and others. Both Christian antisemitism and the structures of political totalitarianism and imperialism that have arisen in Christian history owe their origins to this false assumption of eschatological fulfillment.

Ruether maintains without qualification that the traditional idea of the Christ event as the final Messianic revelation needs to be reformulated. In her published works Ruether thus far has not offered any comprehensive reformulation. She has, however, indicated some general directions which it would need to follow. Her basic inclination would be to understand the Messianic dimensions of Jesus' ministry as having a paradigmatic and anticipatory value. It provides a future vision even though it did not bring about a final completion of human history. Ruether would insist that such an approach demands a significant relativization of the Christ event with respect to other faith traditions which have no direct contact with this paradigmatic experience. The Cross and the Resurrection constitute authentic eschatological paradigms only for the people who have consciously accepted them as such. Others who have turned to alternate paradigms which have emerged compellingly from central experiences in their own respective histories should not be looked upon by Christians as unredeemed. Nor should their faith perspective be termed a false one. "This contextual view of the significance of the Cross and the Resurrection," says Ruether, "takes seriously the diversity of peoples and their histories, out of which they hear God through the memory of different revelatory experiences."[49]

Ruether in fact has written a more lengthy, still unpublished, Christological reformulation in which she carried her ideas somewhat further. Michael McGarry, who had direct access to this manuscript, offers a brief outline of her more developed approach in his volume.[50] She clearly rejects most of the recent attempts at Christological statement by such Christian scholars as Bultmann, Pannenberg and Moltmann. She likewise is unhappy with efforts to develop a Christology of progress on one hand or the notion of Jesus as the "perfect person" on the other.

All she will grant about the Christ event is that it reveals to us something fundamental about the nature of human existence, specifically the point of tension between what actually is and what ought to be. The man Jesus stands as a model of the hope that the ideal is in fact possible of attainment in the future. Christ constitutes the theological symbol for the fulfillment of that hope. Jesus Christ represents the unification of the human community with its ultimate destiny which is yet to come and in whose light men and women can continue to hope and to struggle for the realization of that unity. For Ruether the Christ event also reveals the ultimate overthrow of evil and the establishment of God's reign even though evil still holds sway on many fronts.

The Exodus event, as Ruether interprets it, does the same for Jewish identity that the Christ event does for Christianity. It is the foundation of hope and a statement about the ultimate conquerability of evil. The Christ event in no way invalidates the value of the Exodus experience as a paradigm, nor vice versa. Each speaks to a different group of people.

Ruether's writings have provoked the Christological question in the dialogue in a way no others have. Her contribution is important in boldly challenging the traditional assertions about Jesus' fulfillment of Judaism and in showing forth the shadow side of what she describes as the "historicizing of the eschatological" process. Her insistence that Christian faith must be reanchored in the flow of history should be enthusiastically endorsed.

For now, however, her contribution stops here. While there are certain possibilities in what we know of her positive reformulation of Christology, she has relativized the Christ event far too much. Also, her failure to significantly incorporate insights from Second Temple Judaism into this reformulation has led to an excessively harsh critique of the move to a more "spiritualized" form of Christological interpretation. She only sees the shadows, never the potential light in the process. Finally, in her over-relativization of the Christ event she has failed to indicate whether the revelations in the Exodus and in the Christ event differ in any manner. One does not have to maintain the traditional fulfillment/superiority interpretation of the Christ event relative to Judaism to continue to claim a measure of uniqueness and centrality for it. In fact, without maintaining some uniqueness and centrality for the Christ event there remains little reason to retain Christianity as a distinct religion. This outlook does not exclude the possibility, nonetheless, of also viewing Judaism as a faith tradition with unique and central elements. Each tradition needs to learn from the other. Ruether's Christology, at least as far as she has developed it up to now, remains too minimalist for an authentic Christian self-identity. But, in spite of this reservation, it is important to state that her contribution to the necessary task of Christological reinterpretation has been immensely significant.

Recently, another scholarly volume has opened new dimensions in the double-covenant approach. It is E. P. Sanders' *Paul and Palestinian Judaism* which has all the qualifications to become a classic work.[51] Its only serious limitation with regard to the Christological question is the exclusive reliance on Pauline thought.

Sanders had thoroughly researched Palestinian Judaism in the Second Temple period, in particular its relationship to central theological themes in the writings of Paul. It can be said that no recent Christian scholar has shown as comprehensive and profound an understanding of the Second Temple material as Sanders. This is a definite strength of Sanders' approach.

His research has led Sanders to two principal conclusions: (1) there was a generally prevalent religious outlook in Palestinian Judaism which he calls "covenantal nomism"; (2) the Pauline pattern of religious thought was basically different, focusing its attention on what might be described as "participationist eschatology." Thus Sanders would say that Christianity, at least to the considerable extent that Paul influences its basic theological outlook, is a different type of religion than Judaism. While their practice or theory may be similar in many areas, the basic patterns through which each expresses its faith stance are distinctive. He writes:

> We thus in a way agree with one of the conclusions of previous comparisons of Paul and Judaism, that there are peripheral agreements and a basic disagreement. I should say, however, that there are *substantial* agreements and a basic difference. Further, the difference is not

located in a supposed antithesis of grace and works (on grace and works
there is in fact agreement, and an agreement which can hardly be called
"peripheral"), but in the total type of religion.[52]

Sanders uncovers distinctive features in Pauline thought in several key
areas. Among these are the meaning of righteousness, the role of repen-
tance, the nature of sin, the nature of the saved "group" where Sanders
feels that the "body of Christ" notion is considerably different from
incorporation into the covenant with Israel, and the necessity of a person
transferring from the realm of the damned to that of the saved. In
discussing all these issues Paul moves in directions that are not duplicated
anywhere in the teachings of the Palestinian Judaism of his era.

   Pauline thought as interpreted by Sanders is marked more by a series
of polarities than the smooth sequence characteristic of covenantal nomism. "In Christ" against "in the flesh," "under grace" against "under
law"—these are the types of sharp contrasts in which Paul delights. Basic
to this polarity way of thinking was the conviction that a person through
faith became one with Christ. This union brought about a transfer of
lordship and initiated a personal transformation that would realize matu-
ration only at the end of days.

   As Sanders sees it, the pattern of Paul's faith perspective follows this
outline:

> God has sent Christ to be the Saviour of all, both Jew and Gentile (and
> has called Paul to be the Apostle to the Gentiles); one participates in
> salvation by becoming one person with Christ, dying with him to sin and
> sharing the promise of his resurrection; the transformation, however,
> will not be completed until the Lord returns; meanwhile one who is in
> Christ has been freed from the power of sin and the uncleanness of
> transgression, and his behavior should be determined by his new situa-
> tion; since Christ died to save all, all men must have been under the
> dominion of sin, "in the flesh" as opposed to being in the spirit. It seems
> reasonable to call this way of thinking "participationist eschatology."[53]

Having established his thesis that Pauline Christianity and Rabbinic Judaism constitute two essentially different religious patterns, Sanders quickly
moves on to state clearly his belief that there exists no inherent reason for
considering one pattern superior to the other. It must be said, however,
that Sanders never fully explores the theological implications of this
conclusion. He does observe, however, that the Pauline emphasis on
"participationist eschatology" could not be maintained in its exclusivity in

the post-Pauline church. The faith of the Church was forced more and more to incorporate aspects of "covenantal nomism" into its way of living. But Sanders cautions that this return did not prove Paulinism inferior to Rabbinic Judaism. The preference in Christianity for a form of religious existence grounded in "participationist eschatology" in no way implies that Judaism's continued adherence to "covenantal nomism" was clearly in error. Any number of times Sanders emphasizes that it is wrong to look upon the relationship between Judaism and Christianity in a way that implies an inferior-superior tie. For Sanders the two religious traditions are significantly different. Beyond that he ventures no evaluation of their respective outlooks.

Without being entirely clear on the matter, Sanders appears by implication to grant equal status to both Judaism and Christianity. In so doing he obviously undercuts much of the traditional Christian theology regarding Judaism. Implications regarding the ultimate significance of the Christ event also emerge from Sanders' approach, but he chooses not to elaborate on these.

It is somewhat difficult to link Sanders' approach to other points of view discussed in this chapter. He approaches the question somewhat differently and in a more restricted manner. Since he finally posits Judaism and Christianity as two distinct religions, it is best to include him generally in the double-covenant school. His exclusive concentration on Pauline thought has both negative and positive features. On the negative side, it gives us no clear indication as to where Sanders stands on Pauline Christology over against the Synoptic Christologies on which much of the classical Christian fulfillment theology is based. Sanders does lead us in the right direction, however, in Christological reformulation in emphasizing the developed thought of Paul, but he does not make it clear whether he views Pauline Christology as a later development or whether it represents an acceptable form of Christology over against the Synoptic viewpoint. He likewise remains somewhat ambivalent regarding the continuation of Judaism as a valid religious perspective after the Christ event. In this regard he seems to affirm the view shared by most of the other scholars in the dialogue but in light of the history of the question in the Church it would have helped if he had stated his position more openly and forcefully.

Another positive dimension in Sanders' presentation is his attempt to isolate the unique features in Christianity. He does not try to develop a simple "Christianity is Judaism for the Gentiles" approach. While he concentrates only on Pauline thought, his contibution in this regard is substantial. The one defect is that the contrast between Rabbinic Judaism and Pauline Christianity may be somewhat overdrawn. The "participationist" dimensions of Second Temple Judaism as a basis for covenantal nomism need to be looked at more thoroughly than Sanders has done. His recognition that post-Pauline Christianity had to modify its exclusive dependence on "participationist eschatology" reduces some of the sharpness of the contrast; thus further nuancing of the Sanders model is still demanded. In sum, we can say that rather than presenting any reformulation of Christology in light of the dialogue experience, Sanders' research provides a new base for such reformulation that no serious theologian can ignore.

The last perspective we shall consider under a broadly defined double-covenant category comes from the Swiss biblical scholar Clemens Thoma. His volume *A Christian Theology of Judaism*,[54] while not offering a comprehensive Christology set within a Jewish context, does lay down some crucial ground-rules for such a Christology.

Thoma insists on a point recently made as well by the German scholar Hubert Frankemolle that "Jewish tradition history is not just *one* important presupposition but an integral ingredient for understanding Jesus' meaning in Jewish Christianity."[55] There is simply no way of denying, as has been so frequent in Christian circles, that Jesus and the early Church were profoundly influenced by the progressive form of Second Temple Judaism represented by Pharisaism. Thoma terms Pharisaism the "tap-root" of normative rabbinic Judaism which in turn had a key role in shaping the religious outlook of Jesus and the early Christian community:

> Jesus responded to Pharisaic concerns and arguments and Paul was partly under Pharisaic influence. . . . So-called Early Catholicism, insofar as it found expression in New Testament literature, attempted to bring the Christ event and Pharisaic-rabbinic spirituality and life styles into harmony. Precepts and exhortations in the Deutero-Pauline and Catholic Epistles have many strong parallels in rabbinic writings.[56]

He also makes a point, which will be explicated more fully in the constructive section of this volume (Chapters 4 and 5) that the developed forms of hypostatic Christology have far deeper connections with Rabbinic (Pharisaic) Judaism than with Jewish Hellenism or non-Jewish thought. There are even signs, according to Thoma, that certain Jewish groups partially transferred hypostatic theology to the pre-existent Messiah. The very idea of such a Messiah, in fact, carries Jewish pre-Christian origins.[57] In the end he insists:

> As a Christian observer of the Jewish theological scene, one cannot but conclude that a Christological perception of God—apart from its historical realization—is not un-Jewish.[58]

Thoma recognizes, however, as the data at hand forces us to do, that Jesus did forge an identity in his ministry which separated him in part from the Pharisaic movement with which he otherwise had such close ties. He was likewise not above some harsh criticism of Pharisaism, though in so doing he was frequently merely picking up a strong self-critical dynamic that was characteristic of the movement itself.

The weakness in Thoma's picture is that he does not provide any comprehensive description of how Jesus differed from Pharisaism. He merely offers some hints. One critical area of separation (and hence opposition) between Jesus and the Pharisaic movement *in toto* comes from Jesus' absolute link of "the Kingdom of God to his activities and his person; on this point he was unique. Yet, he was in agreement with the apocalypticists in being deeply imbued with the penetrating assertive power of God in the world."[59] The Pharisees refused to place the approach of God's Kingdom at the heart of their religious teaching. This was an inflammable issue in their encounters with Jesus. The opposition on this point is present not only in the final, redacted sections of the New Testament but in the early materials as well.

Thoma also makes it clear that he does not accept any simplistic view that in proclaiming this Kingdom of God Jesus claimed to be totally fulfilling the Jewish Messianic expectations. Messianic expectation for both Jews and Christians must remain vague and futuristic. He does say, however, that "in Christ the absolute future of God and man became transparent."[60]

Thoma also takes up a major thrust present in the writings of Paul Van Buren: Jesus must be seen as a way to the full experience of the Father God known to the Jews, rather than as in opposition to this God of the Torah. While Jesus did experience this God in a uniquely close and intimate way there are profound links between the Pharisaic conception of God and this experience of Jesus which have been lost sight of by Christians far too often.

While it is difficult to sum up Thoma's final theological position on the Jewish-Christian relationship because it remains somewhat undefined in his volume, it would seem to include the following elements: (1) Christianity is deeply imbedded in Judaism, especially in Pharisaism; even Christology in its more developed forms has roots in the Jewish tradition. (2) The uniqueness of the Christ event is to be found in the proclamation of the Kingdom's presence in the acts of Jesus (and by implication those later performed in his name) and in his intimate experience of God as Father. Hence Christianity has dimensions not present in Judaism. It is not simply Judaism for the Gentiles. (3) The split between Judaism and Christianity, while seemingly not inevitable in Thoma's eyes, did happen. As a result, it appears that in his perspective, while Christianity needs very much to recover its Jewish roots to regain full authenticity, it does represent a sufficiently independent religious outlook to warrant placing Thoma within the school of double-covenant theologians. Based on this, Thoma seems to be close to the approach articulated in greater detail in Chapters 4 and 5.

Some Conclusions

From the above examination of representative Christian scholars with experience in the dialogue it is clear that we are still in the very early stages of the Christological reformulation process. There is not yet any clearly delineated model that has won acceptance from a significant number of reputable scholars. The only areas in which there is general agreement are: (1) that the Christ event did not invalidate the Jewish faith perspective, (2) that Christianity is not superior to Judaism, nor is it the fulfillment of Judaism, as previously maintained, and (3) that Christianity needs to reincorporate dimensions from its original Jewish context, in particular the sense of rootedness in history.

The respective positions advocated by dialogue scholars that (1) Christianity is essentially Judaism for the Gentiles, or (2) that the Christ event is one among several valid Messianic experiences, or (3) that Christianity and Judaism are distinctive religions, each with a unique faith perspective despite their historic links, have each drawn support from several scholars. This volume adopts the position that the most promising and authentic is the third outlook.

A Christology needs to be developed which recognizes central and unique features in the revelation of the Christ event without thereby implying that this represents the totality of revelation. Such a Christology needs to make room both for the ongoing validity of the Jewish covenant and for the recognition of its unique and central insights that presently are not incorporated in a meaningful fashion by the Christian Church. With such a viewpoint it seems that the contributions of Hellwig, Parkes, and Sanders towards Christological reformulation become the most helpful.

Yet we cannot ignore the fact that cumulatively all the scholars we have examined have been responsible for developing a sound basis for discarding the classical understanding of the Christ event with respect to Judaism. Nothing new would be possible without this breakthrough which, one might add, is only beginning to infiltrate mainline Christological thinking in Protestant and Catholic circles and is still almost totally absent in Orthodoxy. This, the universal rejection of previous theological conceptions of the Jewish-Christian relationship by these scholars, represents an historic milestone in Christian theological thinking.

3
Christology and Judaism in Current Systematic Theology

Having sampled some representative Christological viewpoints among Christian scholars with extensive experience in the dialogue with Jews, we shall now examine a select number of major figures in contemporary systematic theology to see how they handle the question of Christology and Judaism. The study of Charlotte Klein referred to in Chapter 1 on anti-Judaism in Christian theology, and another undertaken by Eva Fleischner on German theology since 1945,[61] demonstrate that on the whole mainline Christological thinking has ignored this question or continued to espouse the traditional outlook that the Christ event represents the fulfillment of Judaism pure and simple. Fleischner shows, for example, that such leading figures in the contemporary Christological debate as Johannes Metz, Walter Kasper and Karl Rahner do not even consider the issue.

Very recently, however, there has emerged among a few present-day theologians some awareness that Christology must be rethought relative to its implication for the continuation of the Jewish covenant. Wolfhart Pannenberg, Jürgen Moltmann, Hans Küng and Edward Schillebeeckx are four contemporary systematicians who fall into this category. Several of the exponents of liberation theology, with their stress on the centrality of the Exodus event for Christological interpretation, have also at least indirectly taken up the question. Hence it is important to see where these writers are leading us on the question of Christology and Judaism and how closely their perspectives approach those which have developed among the Christian scholars with deep ties to the dialogue.

European Protestant Perspectives: Pannenberg and Moltmann

One of the first systematicians on the European continent to lift up the Jewish question was Wolfhart Pannenberg. In his major volume *Jesus: God and Man,*[62] he deals at length with the significance of Jesus' death and Resurrection vis-à-vis Judaism. Pannenberg insists that we need to probe deeply the grounds of the conflict between Jesus and the Jewish authorities that led to his eventual execution. When this is done, we shall see that it was not any one incident that brought about his death, but the way he generally placed himself above the Jewish legal tradition and argued that God's authority lay at the heart of his teaching. Blasphemy, based on usurpation of authority properly belonging only to God, was according to Pannenberg the likely reason why the Jewish authorities decided to hand him over to the Roman government for punishment.

Pannenberg feels that the charge of blasphemy leveled against Jesus by the Jewish authorities has a basis if one takes the perspective of the Torah tradition as developed in post-exilic Judaism. It was not just a case of malevolent slander nor merely ill will on the part of his opponents. Neither can Jesus' execution be attributed to the work of a few inadequate individuals. To explain the genesis of Jesus' trial and death on this basis, says Pannenberg, is really to miss the true significance of Calvary.

The Torah system condemned Jesus, as Pannenberg sees it, because he had clearly and consciously set himself above that system. This is Pannenberg's deep conviction:

> The rejection of Jesus was inevitable for the Jew who was loyal to the law so long as he was not prepared to distinguish between the authority of the law and the authority of Israel's God. Jesus certainly did not attack the law formally; but he did place his own authority above that of the words of Moses. It is understandable that this behavior was considered to be blasphemy. . . .
>
> Jesus could come under the curse of the law only if and to the extent that he stood as a transgressor against the law and thereby against God Himself who had given the law. That, however, was in fact the case, since he had set himself above the traditional authority of the law through his claim to authority. This action appeared at the same time to question God Himself as the one who had made known His will in the law. To that extent Jesus' claim to an authority on a par with God inevitably meant blasphemy in the eyes of the Jew who was faithful to the law.[63]

It is only in light of Jesus' Resurrection that the blasphemy situation becomes clarified. If Jesus' Resurrection from the dead is acknowledged to be an act initiated by God himself and this is a divine seal of approval on the activities and teaching of Jesus during his ministry, then the judgment of the Jewish community is seen in its true face. That judgment, not Jesus' teaching, became blasphemy in Pannenberg's perspective.

Thus, for Pannenberg, it becomes essential for Christian self-identity to retain this fundamental conflict between Jesus and the Jewish law in all its sharpness. He is highly critical of any attempts, from either the Christian or the Jewish side, to soften the tension in the name of better inter-religious relations in our day. Jesus did not run into problems merely with the administration of the law, but with the law itself. Until Jesus began his preaching, the Torah represented the valid historical formulation of God's saving activity, even though in Pannenberg's eyes the law had become "calcified" in the Second Temple period. All that changed, however, when Jesus preached a new primacy for the commandment of love rooted in a sense that the eschatological Kingdom of God was indeed near at hand. The validity of the law as traditionally understood was irreparably undercut by this proclamation. Jesus' Resurrection confirmed this proclamation, freeing humankind once and for all from the limitations of the law and totally eroding the foundations of the Jewish religious tradition. As Pannenberg bluntly puts it:

> . . . either Jesus had become a blasphemer or the law of the Jews—and with it Judaism itself as a religion—is done away with. That the latter is the case became clear from the perspective of Jesus' resurrection. Judged in this light the standards are reversed. What previously was blasphemy is now the expression of the highest authority, or true unity with God Himself; what previously seemed to be demanded for the sake of the divine law is now revealed to be blasphemous outrage. Jesus' resurrection cleared away the ambiguity that hung over Jesus' pre-Easter activity. Therefore, the message of freedom from the law results from the perspective of the resurrection.[64]

Pannenberg goes on to develop his Christology in terms of the notion of "substitution." Jesus' death itself takes on for him the character of a service. Regarding Israel, Pannenberg sees the death of Jesus as atoning for the false charge of blasphemy imposed upon him by the Jewish community. The Resurrection showed that Jesus died a righteous man, not a blasphemer. It is also revealed that not only the circle of Jesus' Jewish judges but in principle every Jewish person who accepts the authority of the law falls into the category of blasphemer. Jesus' death/Resurrection has totally reversed all prior standards. The death penalty imposed upon Jesus is in effect the punishment which the whole Jewish people deserved, to the extent that it acquiesced in bondage to the authority of Torah.

But Jesus' death carried vicarious meaning for more than the Jewish people. Not only the Jews, but with them all men and women are disclosed as blasphemers by the Christ event. In part Jesus' conflict with the Roman political power of the day reveals the universal dimension of the Cross/Resurrection. Yet by itself the conflict would not have fully legitimated the universal significance of Jesus' death. Only after it became clear that in his death Jesus experienced the abandonment by God as the result of human attempts to achieve equality with God, and that Jesus' death had eliminated this pride once and for all, can we look upon the Roman procurator in the trial of Jesus as a representative of non-Jewish humanity.

But it is Pauline theology that for Pannenberg confirms the universalistic thrust of Jesus' death. As a result of his death, the Gentiles were able to enter into Israel's history of election. The nullification of law as the sole instrument of God's grace made it possible for Gentiles to attain community with God without accepting the Jewish legal tradition. Freedom from the law is for Paul, however, only a pre-condition for universal sharing in the salvific death of Jesus. The real basis is to be found in the notion that since all have sinned, not just the Jews, all are subject to death. It is this anthropological perspective that Pannenberg contends makes it theologically possible to extend the significance of Jesus' death to all men and women, not just to the Jews. The Jews, revealed as blasphemous by the Resurrection, assume the status of representatives of all humanity standing over against the claims of Jesus. The Cross, in this perspective, constitutes a scandal to both Jews and Gentiles. Paul forges a bond between Jewish law and the more general anthropological link between sin and death. In so doing, it becomes possible in the Pauline perspective to tie Jesus' death to the ultimate fate of all humanity.

That the death/Resurrection of Jesus took place was not due in the final analysis to human insufficiency. The power of God was at work. The judgment over Jesus was authorized by God himself. In his dying, Jesus carried the consequences of separation from God and the punishment for sin, not only in place of his fellow Jews, but as an agent of all humanity. Death has been conquered by Jesus' act of substitution—this is for Pannenberg the very essence of the Christ event:

> Through him . . . the Godforsakenness of death is overcome for all men. No longer must anyone die alone and without hope, for in community

with Jesus the hope for one's own future participation in the new life that has already appeared in Jesus and whose content is community with God has been established.[65]

Such a Christology, while it tries very hard to establish a positive role for Judaism prior to Christ and while it looks upon Jews not as the only sinful people but as representatives of all humankind in its anti-God rebellion, will hardly meet with great approval in a dialogue setting. It obviously leaves no theological space for the Jewish community after the Christ event. As stated in *Jesus: God and Man,* the only positive contribution of Pannenberg's Christology to the dialogue is that it at least seriously raises the question of Judaism, unlike many other contemporary Christologies which totally ignore it. But unfortunately the presentation of Judaism is such that it seems to equate Judaism almost totally with legalism.

Richard John Neuhaus, in his introduction to a subsequent volume by Pannenberg entitled *Theology and the Kingdom of God,* is quite critical of his handling of the Jewish question. Neuhaus writes:

This view of Judaism is highly objectionable and thoroughly disappointing in the light of the suggestiveness of Pannenberg's view of history. Is it not possible that there are several legitimate interpretations of the Hebrew Biblical tradition? ... In his Christology, Pannenberg argues that the resurrection definitely settled the interpretation of pre-Christian Judaism. If it is true that Jewish religion itself collapsed, then what is the Judaism of subsequent centuries and of our own day?[66]

Neuhaus feels that Pannenberg has failed to see the possibility of multiple interpretations of the Jewish religious tradition. If he were willing to acknowledge this, then the one developed by the early Church would not have to be presented as the only viable option for a believing person. While a person could select the Christian faith perspective, the Jewish tradition would remain a valid, rather than a blasphemous, choice as well.

The Jewish theologian Eugene Borowitz is harsher than Neuhaus in his critique of Pannenberg's position. He strongly asserts that any theology which depicts Judaism as having ended two thousand years ago, as Pannenberg's does, reduces Jews to the category of dispensable persons and implies that they have become satanic. Such a theological point of view also opens wide the doors of prejudice and persecution.

Borowitz writes:

> To make Christology again the source of anti-Semitism is to be blind to
> Christian teaching as the preparation for Hitler and the Holocaust. To
> make this a pillar of a religion of love is contemptible. But to be a
> contemporary German and say such things is intolerable. So much
> suffering, so many deaths and the old Jew-hate reasserts itself! Such
> grand theorizing about history and eschatology and no sense that the
> thinker stands on bloody ground and lends the devil a hand.[67]

As a result of visits to the United States where he has engaged in some
scholarly encounters with Jews, Pannenberg has modified his original
position to some degree. He has, for example, indicated agreement with
the perspective offered by Hans Joachim Schoeps in his volume *The
Jewish-Christian Argument.*[68] In that volume Schoeps characterizes the
eschatology of Judaism as revolving about "that which is to come" while
Christian eschatology focuses on the return "of him who has come." Both
faith communities agree that the final Kingdom is yet to come, and only
then will the tension between them be finally resolved. In terms of
Messianism and eschatology, Judaism and Christianity are both provisional forms awaiting the healing truth which still lies ahead.[69]

In the foreword to another more recent work, *The Apostles' Creed in
the Light of Today's Questions,*[70] he clearly acknowledges a change of
viewpoint in several areas from that found in *Jesus: God and Man.* He calls
the alteration regarding the Jewish question the most profound of all the
changes in his original thesis. He attributes his earlier position, in which he
argued that the death/Resurrection of Jesus put an end to the validity of
the Torah and hence in principle to the Jewish religion which was totally
centered in the Law, to the widespread contention in German Protestantism that the religion of the Law and Judaism are identical. He now is of
the opinion that a fundamental distinction can and must be made between
them. He has come to understand that in the Jewish faith perspective the
God of history can stand above the Law. With such an understanding it is
now possible for Pannenberg to describe the activity of Jesus as a totally
Jewish phenomenon. The recognition of the Jewish context of Jesus'
ministry gives the dialogue between Christians and Jews a much greater
potential, since in addition to the contrasts between the two traditions
there also exists a broad common basis.[71]

Pannenberg has also included an "Afterword" in the second edition of *Jesus: God and Man* which calls the reader's attention to the change in perspective found in his work on the Apostles' Creed. But unfortunately the body of the text in the second edition remains as is. The corrective information is confined to a footnote.

What can we say of Pannenberg's Christology relative to the Jewish-Christian encounter? Richard Neuhaus has indicated that with some of the changed direction Pannenberg's work has taken since the original publication of *Jesus: God and Man,* his theology may still provide a solid basis for a new theological assessment of the relationship between Judaism and Christianity because of its emphasis on history and on the future rather than past or present Messianic fulfillment. I cannot really concur in this evaluation as yet. My judgment would be much closer to that meted out by Eugene Borowitz, though Borowitz somewhat moderated his assessment in light of some changes made by Pannenberg.[72] For one thing, Pannenberg has not yet altered the substance of his thought. If his change of perspective is as profound as he hints it is in the Apostles' Creed volume, then the basic text of *Jesus: God and Man* should have been changed in the second edition. Otherwise people will continue to put forward Pannenberg's earlier position.[73] It is also not clear how he would fully restate his new position on Judaism in the light of his endorsement of a viewpoint such as that of Schoeps. Admittedly the eschatological outlook offered by Pannenberg could have positive potential for a reformulated Christology that would allow space for Judaism after the Christ event. Yet the end of Jewish religion as a result of the Resurrection seems so fundamental an idea to the Christological formulation found in *Jesus: God and Man* that there is little hope of utilizing this theology as a basis for such rethinking without a major overhaul which Pannenberg has not yet provided.

Another outstanding name in contemporary Protestant theology is Jürgen Moltmann. In his attempt at a contemporary constructive theology he has acknowledged that the events connected with the Nazi Holocaust have shattered much of his earlier theological thinking. He now strongly maintains that no Christian can offer a valid and meaningful interpretation of Christology for the present day unless that Christology seriously reckons with the implications of Auschwitz. He is the first of the major systematic theologians to grapple with the Holocaust in a profound way.

In one of his more recent works, a major volume entitled *The Crucified God,* he treats the Jewish question extensively, though his general attitude still bears traces of the traditional approach to Gospel and Law which have dominated German Protestant scholarship. His explanation of the trial of Jesus largely centers on the implications of Jesus' abandonment of the legal tradition in Judaism. This perspective bears definite similarities to that espoused by Pannenberg in the original version of *Jesus: God and Man.* The following passage brings out well the basic thrust of Moltmann's exegesis on this score:

> [Jesus'] execution must be seen as a necessary consequence of his conflict with the law. His trial by the guardians of the law was in the broader sense of the term a trial about the will of God, which the law claimed to have codified once and for all. Here the conflict between Jesus and the law was not a dispute about a different will, or the will of a different God, but about the true will of God, which for Jesus was hidden and not revealed by the human concept of the law.[74]

Moltmann goes on to relate the fundamental conflict between Law and Gospel in the teaching of Jesus to the promise associated with Abraham. It is his contention that through the preaching of Jesus this promise of life experienced liberation from the shadow of a legalistic understanding of the Torah. It was given universal applicability to all those who cared to believe, whether Jew or Gentile. Moltmann insists that only the crucified God can instill a sense of freedom into human consciousness that will produce world-shattering effects, for only through the Crucifixion has the natural human fear of death vanished. In this interpretation of the significance of the Cross, Moltmann does not stand too distant from Pannenberg. The Church that was born out of the Crucifixion can be a source of liberation for all men and women, Jews included. Moltmann is willing to grant that the continuing existence of the people Israel as a living faith community is a sign that the full redemption of the world remains a future possibility rather than a present reality. With this outlook Moltmann definitely moves far beyond the position advocated by Pannenberg. The two fundamental differences are these: (1) he clearly supports the idea of Judaism's continuing validity as a religion; (2) he insists that this continuing validity has a direct impact on the Church's eschatological vision.

As Moltmann sees it, Christians share an inescapable solidarity with the people Israel, "not only with the Israel of the Old Testament, but also with the Israel which rightfully exists alongside the Church and which in consequence cannot be abolished."[75] For Moltmann the Church remains incomplete and the Kingdom of God has not yet attained the fullness of revelation so long as the two communities of hope exist side by side. He totally repudiates any Christian theology that would posit Judaism as the outdated "religion of the Law" in contrast to Christianity's focus on a religion of love.

Like Pannenberg, Moltmann's reformulated Christology as developed in *The Crucified God* lifts up Jesus' death/Resurrection as the central facet of the Christian faith perspective. The basis of all Christian hope, the fundamental self-understanding of Christ and the Church, is to be found in the sufferings of Jesus and his subsequent Resurrection. Calvary brought about a genuine revolution in our concept of God, for it showed that God himself must suffer to be truly united with his people. God and suffering are no longer contradictions. This perception of God revealed through the sufferings of Christ makes possible an authentic concept of liberation for Christians. The Resurrection, following the sufferings and death of Jesus, is testimony to the fact that in the end

> ... the executioners will not finally triumph over their victims. It also says that in the end the victims will not triumph over their executioners; the one will triumph who first died for the victims and then also for the executioners, and in so doing revealed a new righteousness which breaks through the vicious circles of hate and vengeance and which from the lost victims and executioners creates a new mankind, with a new humanity. Only where righteousness becomes creative and creates right both for the lawless and for those outside the law, only where creative love changes what is hateful and deserving hate, only where the new man is born who is neither oppressed nor oppresses others can one speak of the true revolution of righteousness and of the righteousness of God.[76]

Because the new understanding of God brought to humankind through the suffering and death of Jesus ended any notion that God dominated his creation, it paved the way for ultimate reconciliation between all people and God. Men and women have been liberated from the fear of domination by God and by other people, which in turn led them to create structures of oppression in their relations with others and to try to overcome God's supposed domination through unbelief and through the excessive use of power. By freely undergoing suffering through his Son, God accomplished the ultimate salvation of his people in the root meaning of the term salvation—healing. The power struggle between God and humankind was now over, at least in principle. And so the healing process, which Moltmann admits will be long in realization, can now begin.

In a subsequent volume called *The Church in the Power of the Spirit: A Contribution to Messianic Ecclesiology,*[77] Moltmann has advanced to some degree his outlook on the role of Judaism in the contemporary salvific process. Of special significance are his new emphasis on the unique solidarity Christians should have with the people Israel, his firm belief that the Church's relationship with Judaism holds a priority above all other external relations, and the conviction that Judaism serves as the foundation for the Church, both past and present. Moltmann does not hesitate to assert that the Church's history of anti-Judaism has been a direct cause of its paganization, so evident during the Nazi period. He makes a strong plea that all triumphalism be eradicated from the Christian theological understanding of Judaism. Concretely this involves a rediscovery of the significance of the Hebrew Scriptures for Christian self-understanding, a new appreciation of the unfulfilled nature of Messianic hope, and the recognition of Israel as a full partner with the Church in the task of human salvation. Israel retains her sacred mission alongside Christianity until the end of days. On this latter point Moltmann does not budge for an instant. To be specially noted is Moltmann's contention that Christian hatred of the supposed "obdurate Jew" constitutes in fact an exercise in Christian self-hatred. Without doubt this volume displays a much deeper understanding and appreciation of the Jewish Torah tradition than is evident in *The Crucified God.* Moltmann clearly condemns all Christian supersessionist doctrines about Judaism. This certainly must be judged a strong point in the theology of this volume. He likewise feels that the re-establishment of the modern State of Israel has placed the Christian-Jewish relationship on an entirely different plane.

From the above brief exposure to the lines of Moltmann's Christology, it is evident that he shows a deep sensitivity for Judaism, both in its biblical expression and in its contemporary form, and to the historic Jewish-Christian relationship that is lacking in the writings of most of his theological colleagues. He has affirmed the continuing validity of Judaism and its role in the process of human salvation after the Christ event. He likewise has condemned Christian triumphalistic and supersessionist theologies of Judaism. Eugene Borowitz shares in this general assessment of Moltmann.[78]

Still, some of the questions raised by A. Roy Eckardt in his perceptive review of Moltmann's Christology remain quite valid. Has Moltmann really provided sound theological grounds for his contention that Judaism exists by right after the Christ event and that therefore Christians have no basis for postulating its abolition?[79] Put another way, do we find in Moltmann a comprehensive theology of Judaism which supports the ongoing, independent existence of Israel as a valid faith community? The final answer to both these questions must be "no," at least for the present. And this represents a real weakness in Moltmann's innovative attempt at Christological reinterpretation. His theology has not yet reached the same depth as his genuine personal sensitivity on the Jewish question. He appears to continue to defend the thesis that, with the second coming of Christ, Christian hope and Jewish hope alike will be brought to completion. At the parousia Christ will reveal himself as the Messiah of Israel. Because of their rejection of Christ, however, Jews will be the last to enter the final Kingdom. Again, in this regard, Eckardt's critique is to the point. He argues that Moltmann has merely tempered, not finally overcome, anti-Judaism in his theological stance. He has postponed the final fulfillment to the end time, but Jews still need Christ to reach the Kingdom. As Eckardt puts it, for Moltmann ". . . the Church *does* constitute the practical replacement of Israel in the work of salvation. The Church remains . . . the (round-about) instrument of the salvation of Israel."[80]

Eckardt also feels that in spite of Moltmann's attack on Christian triumphalism he has not really overcome it in his theology, since he claims that with the parousia of Christ both Christian and Jewish hope will reach fulfillment. Such a hopeful theology, in Eckardt's eyes, simply cannot stand up in the face of Auschwitz. Because of the Holocaust, Eckardt also feels the need to reject Moltmann's interpretation of the Crucifixion. He terms it in reality another pre-Auschwitz theology despite Moltmann's stated desire to take the Holocaust seriously as a theological category. For Eckardt Auschwitz has ruled out any attempt to portray the Crucifixion as "a determinative symbol of redemptive suffering. God is not met on the Cross—even in his 'Godforsakenness.' Once upon a time he may have been met there, but he is not met there any longer."[81]

These latter criticisms on the part of Eckardt are rooted in his conviction that the Resurrection must be eradicated from the Christian theological storehouse. It represents in his mind a massive error in judgment on the part of the Church, as we have noted in Chapter 2. Thus Eckardt has to reject any theology as inadequate which does not endorse a clear repudiation of the Resurrection.

I cannot endorse Eckardt's latter criticism of Moltmann. Though there are definite flaws in his Christology from a dialogical perspective, I feel that Moltmann's concept of the "crucified God" can make a definite contribution to the Christological reformulation that is called for in our day. But it is unsatisfactory standing by itself. Part of its weakness is due to Moltmann's demonstrated lack of acquaintance with developments in the Second Temple period of Judaism. Moltmann's interpretation of Judaism, however, is miles ahead of that offered by Pannenberg. It can be built upon, something that cannot be said of Pannenberg, save for radical surgery. It can contribute to a delineation of the uniqueness of Christianity vis-à-vis Judaism, even though it admittedly makes little or no contribution to an adequate theological articulation of the uniqueness of Judaism vis-à-vis Christianity. We shall return to Moltmann's ideas in subsequent chapters.

European Catholic Perspectives: Küng and Schillebeeckx

Turning to the Catholic scene, we find at least two prominent systematic theologians beginning to seriously ask the meaning of Judaism's continued existence for contemporary Christological formulation. Hans Küng has been in many ways the ground-breaker in this respect. In his widely read volume *On Being a Christian,*[82] Küng maintains in the strongest possible language that after the Nazi Holocaust Christians must clearly admit guilt for the centuries of anti-Judaism within the Church that helped make Auschwitz possible. Thus, along with Moltmann, Küng sees the Holocaust as a decisive turning point in the relationship between Jews and Christians. Küng also stresses the significance of the re-emergence of the modern State of Israel. He calls this rebirth the most important event in Jewish history since the destruction of Jerusalem and its Temple. Auschwitz and Israel have together completely eroded the pseudo-theology of Judaism that has been prevalent for so long a time in the Christian churches. Christian theology can no longer look upon Jews as a cursed people because of their rejection of Jesus. Nor can it deny their present election as a people, something maintained by St. Paul, on the grounds that the Christ event transferred this election to Christianity, the new Israel. Too often the Church has set up artificial barriers between the people Israel and Jesus. For Küng, the present imperative for Christianity is not to try to convert Jews but, in turn, to be converted to a humanitarian and theological encounter with Jews that might provide its members with a new self-understanding.

Küng maintains that Judaism is the indispensable content of Christian theology. Without Judaism there would have been no Christianity. He writes:

> The Gospel of Jesus Christ everywhere quite consciously presupposes the Torah and the Prophets. The Christians too hold that the same God of judgment and grace speaks in both Testaments. This special affinity was the reason why Judaism was not discussed in the earlier chapter on the non-Christian religions, although everything positive that was said there about these religions as ways of salvation holds to a far greater

extent and in a very different way for Judaism. It is not with Buddhism, Hinduism and Confucianism, not even with Islam despite its influence there, but only with Judaism that Christianity has this unique relationship: a relationship of origin, resulting in numerous common structures and values.[83]

Küng does not offer any real Christological reformulation in *On Being a Christian* that tries to define a post-Easter theological role for Judaism. He admits that the theological discussion about Jesus in the Christian-Jewish dialogue will prove most difficult. He suggests that through such conversation it may be possible for Jews to help Christians conduct a new search for the meaning of Jesus *from below*. This would mean that the Church would analyze the significance of his person and ministry today from the standpoint of his Jewish contemporaries. Jews might also enable Christians to better comprehend the central statements about Jesus in the epistles and Gospels, especially his honorific titles which have a deeply Hebraic cast. Küng also feels, however, that Jews, as a result of the dialogue, might be led to rethink the religious significance of Jesus for their own tradition. If Christians and Jews enter their dialogue with the firm conviction that Jesus of Nazareth was both a man and a Jew, Küng believes that the two communities can move along together a good distance. He is sensitive to the possibility that this encounter may eventually bring about a profoundly new understanding of the Christ event:

> ... it may be that in the end the final decision for or against Jesus will yet look rather different from what the long Jewish-Christian dispute might have led us to expect. The only plea we are making at the moment is once more for open-mindness which does not permit the unavoidable pre-conception—Christian or Jewish—to become a pre-judgment. We are not asking for neutrality but certainly for objectivity in the service of the truth. At a time of fundamental reorientation of the relationship between Christians and Jews, we shall have to remain open to all future possibilities.[84]

Despite urging openness to all new possibilities, Küng feels that the distinguishing feature of Christianity—the Christ who is identical with the historic Jesus of Nazareth—can never be lost sight of in the dialogue. For him Christ in the last analysis is authoritative, decisive and archetypal for religious meaning in Christianity. It is he who makes Christianity what it really is. Thus, for the moment at least, Küng appears to be highly uncomfortable with those Christologies which do not retain a clear uniqueness for the Church over against Judaism. By implication he seems to reject the "Christianity is Judaism for the Gentiles" approach examined in the previous chapter.

In a 1975 radio dialogue in Germany with the Orthodox Jewish scholar from Israel, Pinchas Lapide,[85] Küng addresses the question of the differences between Christianity and Judaism a bit more thoroughly than he does in *On Being a Christian.* He reaffirms what he said in the earlier volume—the point of separation between Jews and Christians remains the reality that has divided the two communities from the outset: Jesus as the Christ is rejected by the Jews and accepted by the Christian Church. The exact title under which the Church recognizes Christ is not all-important. The various titles attributed to the risen Christ in the New Testament— Son of God, Son of Man, Lord, etc.—are not decisive in their own right. What is crucial is the acceptance of Jesus as the authoritative standard. For Christian believers Jesus constitutes not merely one among many archetypal beings, but the archetype par excellence. Here lies the basic difference, in Küng's mind, since in Jewish eyes the Law is the authoritative standard and not Jesus of Nazareth. As a result, perhaps as a result of his deep Reformation sympathies, Küng endorses the doctrine of justification by faith espoused in the Pauline writings as a—we might even say *the*—key unlocking the significance of Jesus' mission. He refers to this doctrine as "applied Christology" and as "the critical norm for the correct application of Christology."[86] Küng interprets Paul's teaching on the Law as the culmination of the fundamental message proclaimed by Jesus in the course of his ministry. This orientation puts Küng almost in the same camp as Pannenberg regarding the Law, although Küng displays a far greater sensitivity to the continuity of Judaism than the former.

Küng makes it clear that in his understanding of the meaning of the Christ event the distinguishing feature is that the Christian ethos consists not in concrete commandments but in faith in Christ. All individual precepts or prohibitions in Christianity, some of which have been taken over directly from Judaism, are subordinate to the crucified Jesus Christ and his rule:

> It is then not a question merely of what is moral. The gift and the task coincide under the rule of Jesus Christ; the indicative already contains the imperative. Jesus, to whom we *are* subordinated once and for all in baptism by faith, *must* remain Lord over us.[87]

Over and over again in his Christology Küng highlights the centrality of the person of Jesus. Christ's proclamation and Christian witness remain bound to his person, not merely historically but also essentially. It is the following of Christ that distinguishes members of the Church from those who follow other great leaders or teachers in history. Christians also see Jesus as a teacher, but as something more as well. He is "in person the living, archetypal embodiment of his cause."[88]

In the radio dialogue, Küng stresses that the issue for Christians is not simply to develop a doctrine about Christ, but to follow his example. He is convinced that the entire history of Christian-Jewish relations would have been different if Church members had become practical disciples of Christ and put into practice his loving attitude toward Jews and the Jewish religious tradition, instead of merely disputing with Jews on a theoretical level how the Christ event was to be explained.

Küng's openness to the dialogue with Judaism relative to Christology is to be applauded, as is his general sensitivity to the Nazi Holocaust. But up until now, this sensitivity has not really found its way into the core of his Christology. He does not show much evidence of understanding what was taking place within the Judaism of Jesus' day. His Law/Gospel distinction, while far more positive in its evaluation of Judaism than Pannenberg's, in the last analysis runs into the same problem. Küng has failed to provide any sound justification why Christians should look upon Judaism as a valid religious tradition after Christ. Nor has he indicated what Christians might learn from Judaism and vice versa. Gregory Baum has written that Küng's emphasis on the Law/Gospel conflict leads him to a Christological formulation "little apt to improve the Christian-Jewish dialogue."[89] Baum's judgment may be a bit strong but basically on target. While perhaps in his emphasis on the *person* of Jesus one could establish some ties between Küng's position and the thesis put forward by James Parkes and even E. P. Sanders, nonetheless his contrast of the person of Jesus with the Law takes him in a direction quite different from that which Parkes or Sanders follows.

In consequence, Küng's expressed admiration for Judaism has on the whole remained peripheral to the mainstream of his Christological construction until now. Perhaps one day this will change. Küng's basic sensitivity to Judaism, both biblical and modern, would make him a more likely candidate for such change than some other theologians. But a genuine incorporation of the Jewish ethos into his theology would force Küng to undertake some major revisions in his statement of Christology.

The Dutch Catholic theologian Edward Schillebeeckx, in his volume *Jesus: An Experiment in Christology,*[90] treats the Jewish question at some length. Though he does not show the same broad sensitivity to the tragic features of the historic Jewish-Christian relationship found in Küng, in many ways he treats the subject more comprehensively than the latter. The topic of Judaism continually reappears in his discussions. It should be said that this volume by Schillebeeckx is meant primarily as an examination of exegetical questions and not as a fully developed systematic attempt at Christology. A follow-up volume will be devoted to this task. Therefore any interpretation of the Christological directions offered by Schillebeeckx in this first volume must remain conditional until his more constructive statement appears.

In the early part of *Jesus,* Schillebeeckx examines Jesus' attitude toward the Torah. He rejects any idea that Jesus ever had in mind the abrogation of the Law in virtue of his consciousness of divine authority. Jesus radicalized the Law according to Schillebeeckx, but in so doing he clearly stood in the tradition of the great Hebrew prophets. The radicalism introduced by Jesus into Torah did have a special direction. He demanded that his followers love *all people.* This included even the enemy and the tax collectors and sinners. "In other words," says Schillebeeckx, "Jesus' message of God's rule centered on the well-being of mankind."[91] As Schillebeeckx interprets the radicalization inherent in Jesus' ministry, any specific law tending to block a return to the authoritative relationship to Torah and enhancing people's humanity and liberating God from oppressive imagery could be broken. These passages in the New Testament which depict Jesus as challenging the Torah from his position as the Christ were not part of Jesus' own attitude. Rather than transcending the Law, as most Christian commentators insist Jesus did, the Jesus of Schillebeeckx's theology emerges almost as a rigorist, demanding a return to the full spirit and letter of God's Torah.

One example that Schillebeeckx offers to describe Jesus' approach is the story of the cure of the man with the withered hand on the sabbath, in the Gospel of Mark. His selection of this pericope is interesting since that episode is also central for James Parkes in the development of his individual/community model for distinguishing the unique quality of Christianity and Judaism respectively. For Schillebeeckx the issue in this story is not the miracle, but the sabbath. He is aware that the Pharisaic tradition allowed deviations from the strict prescriptions of the Law for the sake of saving a life. But, he says, the Pharisaic decision here was that there was no emergency involved. Jesus could have aided the already handicapped man on a day other than the sabbath. Jesus' real intent, as Schillebeeckx understands it, went far beyond the life-saving exception permitted by Pharisaism:

> Jesus' criticism of the sabbath rest of Judaism goes beyond the Jewish casuistry regarding this, that or the other emergency. It relativizes the sabbath laws in a radical way: the sabbath rest is interpreted as a "time for doing good," not one for "not being allowed": to help a man in trouble is an action specially suited to the sabbath; for then one is fulfilling the saving will of God, from which the "sabbath law" has sprung. Here again Jesus acts as the prophet from God, the "true teacher of the Law." By his liberating conduct, which is an indictment of prevailing circumstances and conditions of life, Jesus is bringing about what for himself is indeed an explosive situation.[92]

While Schillebeeckx does interpret Jesus' ministry as a liberating one, it is not liberation from the Torah as such. He thereby breaks with most of the other major systematicians, especially in continental Europe, who have depicted Jesus' message of freedom as fundamentally opposed to Torah. Jesus is viewed instead by Schillebeeckx as an authentic Jewish teacher of the Law who expressed the deepest salvific intentions of the Torah: freeing the human person for good. Schillebeeckx understands this ministerial approach on the part of Jesus to be entirely consistent with Jewish interpretations of the Law then current.

Schillebeeckx's work does reveal some serious deficiencies in his understanding of Second Temple Judaism. He makes too sharp a distinction, for example, between Pharisaism and Hellenistic Judaism and fails to adequately appreciate the liberalizing trends within segments of the Pharisaic movement of the time. As a result, he overidentifies Jesus with Hellenistic Judaism. His documentation shows no real contact with major Jewish interpreters of the period. And he certainly lacks the kind of understanding found, for example, in E. P. Sanders' work. He likewise fails to do full justice to the Pharisaic perspective in their dispute with Jesus over the healing of the man on the sabbath, in the way James Parkes has done. Nonetheless it must be said that Schillebeeckx's rejection of the basic Law/Gospel distinction is of paramount importance. The description of the freedom component in Jesus' message, as formulated by Schillebeeckx, has possibilities for development into a reformulated Christology that would give Judaism a meaningful theological existence after the Christ event. Jesus' proclamation of freedom would be seen as in step with, rather than opposed to, other possibilities of freedom previously exposed within Judaism, especially by the prophets. Schillebeeckx's perspective in this regard becomes doubly significant when one recognizes that for him it constitutes, along with Jesus' experience of God as Father, the very essence of the Gospel message.

After the death of Jesus the Church began the process of interpreting the meaning of his ministry for future generations. Schillebeeckx rejects the view that Jesus was initially identified with the dynastic-Davidic Messiah, except in certain sectors of Greek-speaking Jewish Christianity. And even where this identification was applied there was a tendency to subsume it within other prophetic-sapiential eschatological ideas of salvation and to interpret this Messianic conception in a non-national and universal sense. Thus he considers the dynastic-Davidic Christology of minimal value in helping to clarify the Christian interpretations of Jesus' exaltation. In fact, Jesus' earthly ministry went directly against the idea of dynastic-Davidic Messianism. In Schillebeeckx's words,

> ... dynastic-Davidic messianism, with its somewhat triumphal traits, was applied to the risen Jesus only in order to construe the resurrection as exaltation. The dynastic-Davidic "Christ" tradition could not in itself provide any terms of experience to justify proclaiming the deceased Jesus to be, in spite of everything, "the Risen One."[93]

Schillebeeckx's position with regard to the Davidic Messiahship seems to place him in opposition to the scheme proposed by J. Coert Rylaarsdam, discussed in the previous chapter. If Schillebeeckx is correct in his assertion about the relative insignificance of this Messianic conception, then Rylaarsdam's theological model for the relationship between Judaism and Christianity would be seriously undercut.

Schillebeeckx is of the opinion that the Church's theology eventually identified Jesus' person with the prophet of the end time, filled with and anointed by God's Spirit, who would bring the good news of salvation, the word of God's reign, to all peoples. Only this prophetic Messianism, rooted in the notion of a "suffering Messiah" already present in Judaism, had the power to supply the ground and potential conditions for the Church to experience Jesus, after his death, as indeed the risen Messiah. Schillebeeckx's view has certain parallels with that of Jürgen Moltmann, though he does not emphasize the suffering aspect of Jesus' Messiahship quite as much. Nor does he connect it in any way with opposition to Torah, as Moltmann does.

The identification eventually forged with respect to Jesus as prophet of the end time did not come about simply by the selection of one model from among the many existing in Judaism at the time. It had multiple roots: the anointed of God concept, the Son of Man, and the concept of messenger found in Second Isaiah. Thus Schillebeeckx de-emphasizes the importance of this or that Messianic title. The confession of Jesus as the Christ was definitely the result of a mixture of several Messianic models, but in no way did it constitute the creation of a new Messianic vision in total opposition to Judaism. Over and over again in *Jesus,* Schillebeeckx affirms that the earliest Christology in the Church was a totally Jewish phenomenon, and that the basic formative period of Christology worked within the framework of the Judaism of the day. This is indicative of Schillebeeckx's attempt to integrate Judaism into the mainstream of his theological thought in a far more profound fashion than any other major Christian systematician to date.

In addition to interpreting Jesus' ministry as liberation from an overly constrictive view of God, Schillebeeckx's Christology centers around Jesus' sense of God as Abba, Father. For Schillebeeckx the Abba-experience provided Jesus with the source and secret of his being. It served as the overall ground for his message and manner of life. As Schillebeeckx puts it:

> The Abba experience would appear to be the source of the peculiar nature of Jesus' message and conduct, which without this religious experience, or apart from it, would lose the distinctive meaning and content actually conferred on them by Jesus.[94]

This sense of God as Father needs to be understood as the unifying component in all Christological construction. All further Christological titles were basically different ways in which the Christian community tried to articulate this perceived reality in Jesus' life. It might also be noted that there appears to be a link between Schillebeeckx's interpretation of Jesus' Abba experience and E. P. Sanders' delineation of participationist eschatology as the basis of Pauline Christology, outlined in Chapter 2.

Schillebeeckx feels that Jesus in the Gospels uses the term Abba in a much deeper and richer sense than was the case in the Judaism of the time. This claim does not seem to be wholly accurate in view of recent Jewish scholarship, with which Schillebeeckx does not seem familiar. We will go into this question in greater depth in Chapter 4. Jewish scholarship does not invalidate Schillebeeckx's description of Jesus' Abba experience. Rather it shows that developments in the Second Temple period closely parallel the understanding of God as Father that stood at the heart of Jesus' self-understanding.

Schillebeeckx insists that the Gospel narrative makes it clear that Jesus distinguished his relationship with God as Father from the experience of God's fatherhood enjoyed by all believers. The two were interrelated, to be sure; in fact, it was through the person of Jesus that the average believer was able to perceive the fatherhood dimensions of God. But the qualitative difference must be maintained. Jesus never speaks of God as "our Father," except when he is teaching people to pray. He speaks rather of "my Father" and "your Father." The separation, in Schillebeeckx's view, is quite deliberate on Jesus' part.

The Abba experience was not confined to Jesus' interiority; it was outer-directed. It served as the source of his unshaken faith that salvation was assured for all people in the coming of God's reign. Only with this experience as wellspring could Jesus dare to proclaim a message of hope in a calamitous and pain-ridden period of human history. The Jesus of the Gospels is anything but naive. He is quite aware of the contrast between the suffering, violence and oppression present in his midst and his personal intercourse with a God who is benevolent and solicitous for all and will not grant the forces of evil ultimate supremacy over the world. This religious experience of contrast is what informs his conviction that it makes sense to proclaim God's liberating rule which should and can prevail in human history. Thus, says Schillebeeckx,

> ... the Abba experience of Jesus, although meaningful in itself, is not a self-subsistent religious experience, but is also an experience of God as "Father," caring for and offering a future to his children, a God, a Father, who gives a future to the man who from a mundane viewpoint can be vouchsafed no future at all. Out of his Abba experience Jesus is able to bring man a message of hope not inferable from the history of our world, whether in terms of individual or socio-political experiences—although the hope will have to be realized even there.[95]

Schillebeeckx comes on quite strong in asserting that any deletion of this special Abba relationship with God from the interpretation of Jesus' life destroys his message and his whole manner of living. It transforms him into an unhistorical, mythical or symbolic being—what Schillebeeckx terms a "non-Jesus." Nothing remains in such a process but an apocalyptical utopia, and the apocalypticist sees no possibility of good coming from human history. Human history remains essentially negative, and only a remnant will eventually escape. This perspective fundamentally clashes with what Jesus was living and preaching during his lifetime. Out of his Abba experience, he preached a positive hope to men and women. Schillebeeckx's description of the apocalyptic form of Christology bears some resemblance to the "spiritualizing and historicizing of the eschatological" process, to which Rosemary Ruether takes strong exception in her writings and which Schillebeeckx also condemns.

The futuristic orientation which Schillebeeckx describes as flowing from Jesus' experience of God as Father is especially significant for any discussion of Christology in the context of the Christian-Jewish dialogue. While not explicitly rejecting any of the previous interpretations of the Christ event vis-à-vis Judaism, the futuristic emphasis undercuts much of the traditional analyses of Jesus as the fulfillment of the Messianic prophecies of the Hebrew Scriptures, as the one who has brought an end to human history. In light of the way in which the Church has customarily handled the Jewish question theologically, this approach represents an important breakthrough and a starting point for new theological construction.

The one further question that arises for Schillebeeckx is why the Church and Synagogue eventually split in bitterness if Jesus' message is as fundamentally rooted in Judaism as he insists. As he sees it, the break with Judaism, the expulsion from the Synagogue, was the work of certain dominant elements within Palestinian Judaism. Jesus, in fact, remained attractive to significant numbers of Hellenistic Jews. For Schillebeeckx the original conflict between the Church and the Synagogue stems more from the inherent sociology of sectarian movements than from clear-cut doctrinal disagreements. It was not a case of Christianity rebelling against a monolithic Jewish orthodoxy, as Christian scholars have frequently claimed.

The Church developed its interpretation of Jesus largely within the parameters of Second Temple Judaism. Yet, the destruction of the Temple at Jerusalem and attempts by the rabbinic leadership to impose some unity within Palestinian Judaism in the hope of surviving the destruction exacerbated differences already present within the Synagogue. Christianity, far from united, found itself in conflict with an emergent Jewish orthodoxy, as did some of the other sectarian movements within the period. The polemics of Paul, the passionate convert, were a preview of what would become a sectarian pattern in the canonical literature of the New Testament: Christianity struggling to firm up its distinctive identity apart from other Jewish groups by insisting that it had the only authentic understanding of the Hebrew Scriptures.

Thus goes the perspective offered by Schillebeeckx. Christianity in its origins reflects the tensions within the Jewish community in which it arose. In its polemics against other Jewish movements of the time Christianity may have buried important parts of its original religious heritage. This is another especially pertinent observation by Schillebeeckx from a dialogical point of view. It opens the doors for the claim that Judaism has preserved certain key notions of human salvation that were blotted out in the Church after its split with the Synagogue, or at least were greatly played down. The need to appear different and superior, a feature common to most sectarian movements, may account at least in part for the increasing shift toward a triumphal ecclesiology and a shift away from Jewish models for speaking about the relationship between Jesus and God in favor of Greek ones, a process culminating in the Christological decrees of the Council of Chalcedon. These models would unfortunately become the touchstone for much of the subsequent antisemitism that has plagued Christianity.

In commenting on the appropriateness of Schillebeeckx's Christology for the Christian-Jewish dialogue, Robert Schreiter makes it clear that in this Christology the sharpness of the polemic against the Jews only makes sense in view of "the shared roots of two estranged brothers."[96] Schreiter goes on to offer several concrete suggestions how Schillebeeckx's overall theological stance might be useful for a dialogical Christology. First of all, by concentrating on the sociological dimension of first-century relations between Church and Synagogue rather than on the doctrinal aspects, it may be possible to view the surface level polemics in the writings involved as somewhat unsuccessful efforts to mediate the human tension involved in such contraries as the Torah of the heart versus the Torah of ritual, or following tradition meticulously over against a desire to go beyond it. Secondly, Schillebeeckx's suggestion that we must take statements about Christian fulfillment as anticipatory instead of participatory with regard to the reign of God allows space for a new discussion of such central Christian concepts as Messiah, salvation and eschatology. Finally, if we understand the anti-Judaic strain in Christology as flowing in part, at least, from the Church's inability to face up to the historical failure of Jesus' preaching of the reign of God (which Schillebeeckx understands as one of the poles of Jesus' ministry), we might be in a good position to turn around such anti-Judaism by approaching this "failure-in-meaning" in a new way. Rather than simply trying to cover up such failure by projecting the fulfillment of God's reign to a non-historical sphere, we might come to appreciate that this failure clears the ground for the emergence of other faith meanings. Using this interpretative tool with respect to anti-Judaic texts will open the door, Schreiter believes, for the creation of a new theology of Judaism.

It is certainly encouraging to find such a major figure in contemporary theology as Schillebeeckx sensitive to the historic tension between Judaism and Christianity. His stress on the tension as more sociological than doctrinal is a welcome contribution to the discussion of the question. The same may be said for the theological method he suggests for handling the polemic texts. He lays firm ground for the possibility of building a new theology of Judaism in the Church that need not be totally bound by the surface meaning of the classical texts. This in itself represents a major breakthrough in theological methodology.

Still, it must be honestly stated that Schillebeeckx, like Küng, avoids some of the central issues about the meaning of the Christ event vis-à-vis the continuing validity of Judaism. Does Christianity possess an essential content of salvation which Judaism lacks? Is Christ meant ultimately to be the savior of the Jews, as Moltmann implies? In this regard Schillebeeckx, who shares with Moltmann a belief in the anticipatory nature of the proclamation about the presence of God's reign, is much more vague than Moltmann in spelling out the ultimate implications of this position. Because of this lack of clarity in Schillebeeckx's Christology, it is difficult to know whether A. Roy Eckardt's critique of Moltmann could have application to Schillebeeckx's position as well. It can also be asked whether Judaism contains essential revelatory elements that need to be incorporated into the Christian understanding of human salvation. Given the fact that Schillebeeckx acknowledges that the Church may have lost some important ingredients of its Jewish heritage when it separated itself from the Synagogue, there may be room in his thought for a positive answer to this question and hence constructive theological space for Judaism in the post-Easter period. Finally, Schillebeeckx is not clear whether Judaism after Christ can have experiences that parallel the Abba experience of Jesus. Also, what is the present status of the pre-Christian biblical experiences of Israel which he admits were of a kind, though of a different mode, compared to those found in the life of Jesus? Hopefully, Schillebeeckx will one day address this question directly. There is little doubt in my mind that of the major European systematicians his writings contain the best base for building a new theology of Judaism in the Church.

Latin American Perspectives

Besides the European systematicians, another group of theologians exercising an increasingly significant influence on the shape of contemporary Christology are the Latin American liberation theologians. While all of them have their own particular way of addressing the Christological question, they are united in several concerns, among them the need to make praxis the basis of theological construction, the significance of history for establishing authentic religious meaning in our time and the importance of the communal dimension of Christian living.

Few of the liberation theologians have grappled in any profound fashion with the Jewish question respective to Christology. This is certainly a crying weakness in their thought. Yet, because of their growing role in the Christian churches and the fact that some of them have made themes like the Exodus event central to their systematic theology, it is necessary for us to take a brief look at representative samples of their work. We shall focus on four current theologians in this group: Gustavo Gutierrez and José Miguez Bonino, two of the early liberation theologians in terms of international recognition, and Jon Sobrino and Leonardo Boff, whose works are only beginning to have an impact outside of their own continent.

We begin with Gustavo Gutierrez whose *A Theology of Liberation*[97] more than any other single work catapulted the Latin American perspective onto the worldwide theological scene. His specific treatment of Judaism occurs in the discussion of two questions central to his theology: (1) the significance of the Exodus event for human salvation and political liberation, and (2) Jesus' relationship to the revolutionary political movements of his day. In both areas Gutierrez shows some sophistication relative to the realities of Judaism, especially if compared to classic Christian theological portrayals. Nonetheless, there still remains a serious lack of acquaintance with aspects of Second Temple Judaism, in particular, which results in a continuing theological distortion of Judaism.

For Gutierrez, any authentic theology of liberation must link itself to the experience of Israel's emancipation from slavery in Egypt, as described and interpreted in the Hebrew Scriptures. As he views it, Israel's liberation from Egypt is an integral part of God's creative activity. The Exodus event is as fundamental and central to the salvific plan for humanity as the very divine act through which the world and its inhabitants came into existence. Gutierrez terms the liberation of the people Israel a political act which allowed them to break out of a situation in which exploitation and misery prevailed and gave them the opportunity to construct a just and fraternal social order. The Exodus event suppressed the existing disorder and helped in the creation of a new order.

Yahweh helped prick the consciousness of Moses, enabling him to comprehend his vocation as the liberator of the Jewish people. Perceiving his call, Moses worked long and hard to bring Israel out of bondage. The process would take time, for, as Gutierrez puts it:

> A gradual pedagogy of successes and failures would be necessary for the Jewish people to become aware of the roots in their oppression, to struggle against it, and to perceive the profound sense of the liberation to which they were called. The Creator of the world is the Creator and Liberator of Israel, to whom he entrusts the mission of establishing justice. . . .[98]

The Exodus thus represents for Gutierrez a fact of history and a fact of salvation which fundamentally shaped the faith of the Jewish people. Through this act of political liberation Yahweh demonstrated his profound love for his people who in turn received the gift of total liberation.

Gutierrez also ties the Exodus directly to Israel's covenantal tradition. For him, the covenant and the liberation from Egypt constitute different dimensions of the same basic movement, a movement whose end result was a profound encounter with the Creator God. The Exodus event inaugurated Israel's salvific history, made possible through the covenant. The meaning of this creative act of liberation on the part of Yahweh will be remembered throughout the history of Israel, a history in which the Jewish people experience continual re-creation. The God who transformed the primitive chaos into the beautiful world of the cosmos is the very same God who delivers Israel from a situation of alienation to one marked by liberation.

It is against the background of the Exodus experience that Gutierrez begins to develop his Christology. He ties the work of Christ directly to the movement of salvation/liberation that the Exodus launched. In fact, he claims that the redemptive activity of Christ brings the liberating process to its complete fulfillment. The activity of Christ constitutes a new creation. This creative activity is again linked to a liberation which, in Gutierrez's words,

> . . . fulfills in an unexpected way the promises of the prophets and creates a new chosen people, which this time includes all humanity. Creation and salvation, therefore, have in the first place a Christological

sense: all things have been created in Christ, all things have been saved in him.[99]

Because of the connection he establishes between the Exodus event and the Christ event, Gutierrez also interprets the Christian Eucharist in terms of the Jewish Passover tradition. He stresses the thorough Jewish background of the Eucharist as the meal which reveals the full meaning of the Jewish Passover tradition. The Eucharistic rite in its essential elements has a communitarian dimension. It is meant to develop a human brotherhood just as the Exodus experience and its continued remembrance in the Passover forged the Jews into a peoplehood.

In connection with his treatment of the Exodus experience, Gutierrez raises the question of the eschatological promises made by God throughout the course of human history. The first of these was the covenant which, as we have seen, he has already intimately linked with the Exodus liberation. Falling into very traditional Christian language regarding Judaism, Gutierrez says that since the

> ... infidelities of the Jewish people made the Old Covenant invalid, the Promise was incarnated both in the proclamation of a New Covenant, which was awaited and sustained by the "remnant," as well as in the promises which prepared and accompanied its advent. The promise enters upon "the last days" with the proclamation in the New Testament of the gift of the Kingdom of God.[100]

Yet, in spite of his rather traditional approach to the question of fulfillment, there is a potential saving feature in Gutierrez's position. The ultimate future salvation, the promise as he calls it, is announced but only partially fulfilled even in the Christ event. There continues to exist what Gutierrez terms a dialectical relationship between the final promise and its partial fulfillment. The Resurrection has not totally completed the work of Christ. In some ways the resurrected Christ remains "future to himself." With the Incarnation, the self-communication of God with his people entered a decisive stage, but the fullness of that communication still lies ahead. For Gutierrez it is clear that the New Testament story is the realization of the promise only incipiently, and the human community, through its self-generation within the historical process, continues to play a vital and direct part in the ultimate realization of this promise.

This understanding of the still "unfulfilled" nature of the promise leads Gutierrez into arguing for what he calls the "uncentering" of the

Church. For him, this means that "the Church must cease considering itself as the exclusive place of salvation and orient itself toward a new and radical service of people."[101] Too often, he feels, to be for or against Christ too easily becomes identified with a person's allegiance to the Church. Christians lose their ability to discover fragments of the truth beyond the frontiers of the Church. While Gutierrez, without doubt, emphasizes the universal dimensions in the Christ event, his hesitation on the "fulfill-ment" question and his recognition of the presence of authentic religious meaning outside the boundaries of the Christian Church seem to open up the possibility for some continuing post-Easter role for Judaism, along with other non-Christian religions—despite his regrettable regression, on occasion, into classic Christian stereotypes of Judaism's role. But Gutier-rez has unfortunately not developed this perspective in any explicit way relative to Judaism.

The second place where the discussion of Judaism enters rather significantly into Gutierrez's thought is his treatment of Jesus' revolution-ary outlook. He takes the position that Jesus was not a political revolution-ary in the Zealot sense. The outlook of the Zealots was too restricted. It looked down upon such groups as the Samaritans and the pagans, while Jesus' message was addressed to all men and women whatever their station in life. The justice he preached knew no natural boundaries. Jesus also taught a much more spiritual approach to the Law while the Zealots were fierce defenders of its literal observance.

Yet Gutierrez insists that the question of Jesus and concrete political activity cannot stop with a denial of his Zealot associations. There is little doubt that Jesus confronted head-on the groups in power within the Judaism of the period. This included, according to Gutierrez, the publi-cans, the Sadducees, and the Pharisees. With respect to the last of these groups, the Pharisees, Jesus shared with them a distaste for the oppressive domination represented by the Roman imperial authority. But he could not go along with the complex world of religious precepts and norms of behavior they had constructed in order to live on the margins of that domination in a spirit of co-existence. Jesus, says Gutierrez, lashed out against the very foundations of the Pharisaic machinations regarding the Law. In unmasking the falsity of their stance he assumed the role of a dangerous traitor in their eyes. Gutierrez, however, does not fall into the traditional Christian assertion that the Jews were responsible for the death of Christ, even though he understands Jesus as fundamentally in opposi-tion to all the major Jewish groups of his time.

Further discussing the relationship between the Zealot revolutionaries and Jesus, Gutierrez insists that the former were not off base in feeling that they stood in a paradoxical situation relative to Jesus. They sensed that he, too, stood for the liberation of the Jewish people. But they also recognized that he spoke of a revolution more universal and permanent than they were prepared to acknowledge. Gutierrez understands Jesus' liberation of the Jewish people as only one facet of a much wider revolutionary struggle. It would be totally inaccurate in his view to claim that Jesus showed no interest in Israel's liberation. On the contrary, he exhibited keen interest in it, while at the same time placing it "on a deeper level with far-reaching consequences."[102]

The leaders of the other Jewish groups in Jesus' day and the Roman authorities who were responsible for his execution were likewise not mistaken in thinking that Jesus posed a threat to their hegemony. They were mistaken, as are their followers today in Gutierrez's eyes, only in the belief that the impact of Jesus' teaching and ministry would quickly fade after his death. They failed to understand the true source of the Gospel's political dimensions, the nucleus of its transforming power. If the message of Jesus has a subversive quality, says Gutierrez, it is due to its appropriation of Israel's life. The Gospel provided that life of Israel with its deepest meaning. The life and preaching of Jesus posit the unending search for a new kind of human person who will live in a qualitatively different social milieu in which justice predominates and the possibility of communion with God is opened up to all people.

With respect to the question of Christology and Judaism, the position of Gustavo Gutierrez can only be assessed as a mixed blessing. It is encouraging to find missing from his work some of the classic stereotypes of Judaism, such as those connected with responsibility for the death of Jesus. His attempt to link the Exodus and the Christ event has definite possibilities for further development, and his emphasis on history as the unfulfilled side of the promise will find a genuine resonance within Jewish religious tradition. While he has far from an adequate understanding of the Torah tradition in Judaism, he at least avoids framing his understanding of the liberation to be found in the Christ event around the notion of freedom from Jewish legalism in the way that Pannenberg, Moltmann and Küng do. Yet, enough of the traditional outlook in the Church regarding the invalidity of Judaism after Christ has crept into *A Theology of Liberation* to merit severe criticism of Gutierrez on this score. He has not really grappled seriously enough with the ongoing meaning of Jewish religious existence for Christological interpretation. He has likewise failed to apply his principle about the fragments of truth to be found outside the Church to the situation of post-Easter Judaism. He lacks any thorough knowledge of the Pharisaic movement, a condition that leads him to portray this group and their relationship to Jesus in the usual derogatory manner, a depiction incidentally condemned by the 1975 Vatican Guidelines for Catholic-Jewish Relations.

As a summary judgment, I would have to say that despite its severe limitations, Gutierrez's position has the possibility of being transformed into a Christology that could allow authentic theological space for Judaism. Admittedly, this would not be easy and would require some wholesale changes that Gutierrez himself might very well consider an abandonment of his basic thesis. Though he does not show the same concrete sensitivity to Judaism that Schillebeeckx does, Gutierrez's work approaches the same usefulness as Schillebeeckx's for the construction of a contemporary Christology that would not invalidate Judaism. It appears that, unlike many of the European theologies we have considered, the stereotypes of Judaism remaining in Gutierrez's writings are not *pivotal* for his Christology. That is, they could be dropped without asking Gutierrez to totally alter his explanation of the meaning of the Christ event in terms of liberation. Thus, in the world of contemporary Christologies, Gutierrez's provides us with at least a ray of hope for dealing with the Jewish question in a constructive fashion. It may not appear so at first glance, since some of the classic stereotypes leap out at the reader. Still, a more sober analysis will show that the identification of the Exodus event with the Christ event as fundamental moments in the liberation process leading to the single promise opens some new doors for constructive theology. The real question that remains unanswered with Gutierrez—and it is without doubt a crucial question—is whether the Exodus event remains a liberating event for Jews in the post-Easter period in light of their unwillingness to accept the Christ event as liberating. Gutierrez's sympathetic use of Jewish authors relative to the explanation of the Passover's meaning might hint that he would answer the question affirmatively. Clarification of this issue, however, constitutes one of the first steps needed in order to depict Gutierrez's Christology as truly ground-breaking in terms of the Christian-Jewish relationship, a Christology that could authentically serve as the foundation for further development.

In any reading of Gutierrez's Christology, it will also be necessary to take into account the remarks of a Jewish commentator on liberation theology such as Leon Klenicki. He feels that from a Jewish perspective Gutierrez's understanding of the Exodus is too one-sided. He writes:

> Judaism recognizes that it (i.e., the Exodus) was a movement of liberation, but sustains that the liberation from Egyptian bondage became meaningful only when Israel received the Law at Mount Sinai and the Promised Land. The process that starts with Moses taking out an enslaved community culminated with the spiritual liberation of Israel at Mount Sinai, and the possession of Eretz Israel.[103]

Klenicki adds that Gutierrez's volume leaves the reader with the distinct impression that the Jewish people disappeared after the destruction of the Temple. There is much truth in this statement. It is an impression that Gutierrez desperately needs to confront in future writings.

José Miguez Bonino's writings have never reached the comprehensiveness found in Gutierrez. In fact, he does not offer us a Christology per se, but as the principal Protestant exponent of the Latin American theology of liberation, his views, even if not highly developed, bear scrutiny.

In his volume *Revolutionary Theology Comes of Age*[104] he gives a sketch of his approach to liberation theology. It centers around what he calls messianic humanism, a term meant to contrast with humanist Messianism where the exclusive emphasis in politics falls on the activity of the human community. In Bonino's version of liberation theology there is a politics of God as well as human politics. It was first manifested in the Exodus event in which the Scriptures make it clear that Israel conceived of its emancipation from Egypt as due to the activity of God and not merely its own effort. God's power broke through a "closed future" for the Jewish people, brought on by Egypt's oppressive power which led to a "slave consciousness" among the chosen people. This future was suddenly opened by the action of God who showed himself free from the determinism of history.

Much in the same manner as Gutierrez, Bonino establishes a link between the liberating action unlocked in the Exodus event and the freedom offered by the Christ event. He writes:

> Christian hope, far from taking the place of political action, invites and demands that action in the present, in favor of the oppressed, in the light and direction of the promised future. This is the language of the Gospel. The community which enters this action, requires this consciousness, and uses this language as God's People, in continuity with the experi-

ence of Israel and the New Testament—whether they stay within or more outside the visible ecclesiastical institutions. For an engagement with man's liberation and a pressing for God's future are the true marks of the Church.[105]

Insofar as Bonino's outlook parallels that of Gutierrez, it merits the same positive and negative assessment applied to the latter. However, since his thought is not nearly as developed, all judgments must remain somewhat tentative.

Speaking about the nature of the Church toward the end of *Revolutionary Theology Comes of Age* Bonino introduces some ideas which appear to bear upon the Christian-Jewish relationship. He feels that in constructing a theology of liberation it might prove beneficial for theologians to pick up on the distinction between the "covenant of creation" and the "covenant of redemption" found in the Reformed tradition of Protestantism. As Bonino would interpret this tradition, humankind finds itself situated in a realm of responsibility which embraces a threefold free relationship. This relationship includes the human family, the world of nature, and Yahweh, the God of the covenant. Says Bonino:

> The Christian dispensation will then be understood in relation to such a covenant as God's active will to restore man's relationships and responsibility, to reinstate him in his position as partner in the covenant of creation, to put him back again on the road of his self-realization.[106]

The distinct advantage that Bonino sees in the above approach is that it makes room for the soteriological without downgrading the creational dimension of Christianity. Christ becomes something more than a mere step in the progressive evolution of history. Bonino insists that any authentic Christology that stresses the soteriological function of Jesus' coming must be carefully placed within the dynamic perspective so characteristic of the Hebrew Scriptures. If the worlds of creation, both human and subhuman, come to be viewed as static, unchangeable realities, then the Christian myth of salvation of necessity takes on a purely restorational significance (the two-story view) or becomes wedded to a supra-historical realm (the two-kingdoms notion) that reduces the world to the status of a salvific roadblock. But Bonino insists that if the Church would

> ... take seriously the dynamic dimension inherent in the covenant/prophetic theology, the picture is altogether different. Creation is the installation of a movement; it is an invitation and a command to man to

create his own history and culture, creatively to transform the world and make it into his own house and to explore the configuration of human relationships available to him.[107]

Jesus' role in the Christological sketch offered by Bonino is not to super-impose a different, transcendent, or heavenly reality upon nature and history. Rather, he reopens for the human community the will and the power to fulfill its vocational destiny. Bonino admits that such a vocational outlook involves granting the Christian dispensation a certain provisionality and temporariness:

> Jesus' freedom before God, his love for men, his power over nature are not an end in themselves, nor a merely substitutionary activity on our behalf but a truly representational function, in order that and until we ourselves may assume such relationships.[108]

Faith in Christ for Bonino does not mean taking a step beyond humanity but rather toward its full realization. People are Christian in order to be truly human, not vice versa. In the order of salvation, the institutional Church bears a distinctive but clearly provisional and subordinate role. The Church gives authentic witness to the saving activity of God in Jesus Christ when it makes clear the renewed authorization, command and liberation given to men and women to become truly human, to shape their own history and culture, to live and to transform the world, to claim and to exercise the glorious freedom of the children of God. The distinctiveness to be found in the Church lies in its contention that the fullness of humanity is present in the explicit, faithful, and grateful acknowledgement of Jesus Christ.

As a result of this perspective, Bonino says that the response of Christians to those outside the institutional Church who give examples of selflessness, generosity and faithfulness in the historical process must be humility and praise. In a sense, all of us still live in pre-history. While the Church has the responsibility of proclaiming what the period after pre-history will look like, this proclamation is in one sense secondary to the actual doing of salvific liberation. Proclamation without performance becomes not only useless but vain in the extreme. Therefore, the non-Christian who embraces the same liberating historical praxis that is central to any genuine interpretation of the Christ event is on equal footing with Christians even though he/she might not be able to proclaim the ultimate shape of the Kingdom in the same way as believers.

From the standpoint of the Christian-Jewish dialogue, there are several questions one would like to pose to Bonino. What, for example, is the force of the term "renewed" when applied to the liberating effect of the Christ event? Does it, or does it not, imply that the power originally given in the Exodus covenant has grown cold? Or does Bonino mean to imply that it represents a new burst of power without maintaining the end or death of the liberating power inherent in the Exodus? On this issue Bonino is less clear than Gutierrez who more directly ties himself to the traditional Christian stereotype that Second Temple Judaism had lost the liberating spirit of the earlier covenantal/prophetic tradition. Only in one place does he even seem to hint at this old stereotype—in the quotation cited above in which he speaks of the Christian dispensation in terms of "God's active will to *restore* man's relationships and responsibility." The frequent use of the term "renew" relative to the Christ event may be highly significant. For "renew" need not imply the end of the covenantal tradition of Judaism. In fact, it would be quite in keeping with the Jewish vision. The fact that Bonino nowhere describes the meaning of Christ in terms of opposition to the Torah is another significant achievement, especially from a person representing the Protestant tradition where this motif has been so central. There are definite similarities between Bonino's Christological sketch and the position developed by E. P. Sanders, described in the previous chapter. Bonino's stress on pre-history, on the role of those outside the Church in the salvation process, and on the covenantal responsibility for creation would also make his thought more amenable to the ethos of Judaism than most classical Protestant Christologies.

Yet the fact that Bonino never explicitly relates the significance of Jesus to the Jewish tradition is a definite drawback. Several of his statements, when read by a person with traditional bias regarding Judaism, would likely reinforce many stereotypes. It may be that such a person would in fact be misrepresenting Bonino's thought. But only a direct discussion of the question by Bonino would allow us to know for certain where he would situate post-Easter Judaism in his conception of the role of non-believers in the salvific process.

Turning to a third representative of the liberation theology school, we encounter the writings of Jon Sobrino, S.J. His volume, *Christology at the Crossroads,*[109] has brought him to the attention of people outside of the Latin American continent, where his earlier writings have been known for some time. Reading through his extended discussion of Christology from the perspective of the Christian-Jewish dialogue leaves one in a state of total discomfort. It is as though nothing had happened in the Christian theology of Judaism since Vatican Council II. Sobrino almost builds his entire understanding of the freedom and liberation inherent in the Christ event on its contrast with the degraded form of Judaism present in Jesus' day. No better example could be found for Charlotte Klein's thesis about the anti-Judaism so prevalent in Christian theology. It is truly amazing that a Christology so unaware of developments during the Second Temple period in Judaism and their influence on setting the context for early Christianity could still be produced in our day. Without doubt, from the standpoint of an appreciation of Judaism, Sobrino's Christology is one of the worst contemporary examples.

Over and over again throughout the volume Sobrino depicts Judaism in Jesus' day as totally inadequate, and nowhere does he attempt to relate the saving experience of the Christ event in a positive fashion to the saving experience of the Exodus, as Gutierrez and Bonino try to do. Typical of his outlook are the following comments. He insists that the poor "must believe that God is infinitely greater than the God preached by priests and rabbis."[110] Those with whom Jesus debated, says Sobrino, had all imagined "that they had God neatly boxed in their tradition."[111]

While Sobrino does claim that Jesus was a religious reformer who preached the best traditions of Israel, the clear implication is given that Jesus' teachings alone represented this tradition in his own time. Sobrino claims that the exile experience of Israel gave rise to the idea that the faith it had known thus far was without value. He writes:

> This series of negative experiences, pondered in the light of Israel's faith in Yahweh, gave rise to the conviction that it could not be the last word about Israel. There had to be some other possibility because it certainly was not the ultimate that Yahweh could do. There arose the eschatological hope of a complete change in Israel's situation. The Hebrew people began to look forward to some authentic liberation and to a Messiah who would fulfill their hopes.[112]

This interpretation of Israel's exilic experience is never put into the positive context of the Exodus covenant. What Sobrino seems to be saying is that this whole covenantal tradition can only be assessed as negative by the Christian believer; the Christ event really destroyed any value or purpose it might have had previously.

Sobrino accepts without qualification the various anathemas that Jesus hurls against "the Pharisees" in the Gospels. He shows absolutely no awareness of the new scholarship in this regard. This is really difficult to understand in light of his call for beginning Christianity with the historical Jesus. His "historical Jesus" unfortunately must be judged very unhistorical in light of the new scholarship at hand regarding the Pharisees.

Throughout the volume the Pharisees are viewed as prototypes of the legalistic tradition. They are committed to the strict fulfillment of the Law to which Jesus' message of grace and the in-breaking of the Kingdom is totally opposed. Sobrino shows no appreciation whatsoever of the Torah tradition in Jesus' day and the opening up of this tradition which the Pharisaic revolution represented. We shall look at this Pharisaic revolution in greater detail in Chapter 4.

Sobrino contrasts the teaching of Jesus and his disciples with that of Jewish orthodoxy, which must of necessity be called into question. Authentic discipleship in his perspective is the very antithesis of what Second Temple Judaism represented. While perhaps not quite as explicit on the matter as Pannenberg, Sobrino's freedom Christology bears some of the same scars. The freedom that Jesus provides in the knowledge of God and in action for justice stands in direct opposition to Torah. This, the meaning of the Christ event, is predicated on the abolition of the religious system that the Law represented.

In a chapter devoted to the prayer of Jesus, Sobrino further reveals the deep anti-Judaism inherent in his theology. While acknowledging that Jesus knew and used the traditional prayers of his own people, he centers his whole discussion of the theme around the parable of the Pharisees and the publican in the version found in the Gospel of Luke. The Gospel story of one Pharisee is extended by Sobrino to exemplify the prayer of all Pharisees and, by implication, the prayer of all Jews of the period.

In the discussion of the prayer of Jesus, Sobrino never mentions Jesus' best known prayer—the "Our Father." This prayer is profoundly Jewish in its content and would counter the stereotype of Jewish prayer that Sobrino builds out of the parable of the praying Pharisee and the publican. Sobrino's neglect of it is rather mystifying. Its emphasis on the transcendence of God and its petition that God's Kingdom come on earth would seem to be in perfect harmony with the liberationist perspective. "What prayer," asks Clark Williamson of the Christian Theological Seminary in commenting on Sobrino, "could be more authentic from the criterion of liberating praxis? Yet what prayer is more Jewish? Perhaps that is the problem—it doesn't fit Sobrino's anti-Jewish *gestalt.*"[113]

Another disturbing aspect of Sobrino's Christology is his handling of the death of Jesus. He seems to come very close to the traditional accusation that the Jews were responsible for the death of Jesus, a view which Vatican Council II and many national and international Protestant documents have clearly repudiated. His seventh thesis on the death of Jesus maintains that Jesus was condemned to death for blasphemy. Though Sobrino admits that the imperial authorities were directly responsible for his actual execution, the real reason for his death was his opposition to all the Jewish leadership of the period. Sobrino uncritically accepts Mark's account as straightforward history. At the bottom of Jesus' ongoing conflict with the Jewish religious authorities that brought him the death sentence was "his particular conception of God. . . . In the last analysis Jesus is hostile to the religious leaders of his day and is eventually condemned because of his conception of God."[114]

The Pharisees, whom Sobrino on many occasions erroneously equates with the Jewish authorities, have a notion of God that is too confined to the Temple. The God of Jesus is distinct from and greater than the God of the Pharisees. "In Jesus' eyes," he says, "the privileged locale of access to God is people themselves." Sobrino is unaware that the emphasis on the indwelling of God in people in fact constituted one of the principal themes of the Pharisaic revolution. It only goes to show how ignorance of Second Temple Judaism on the part of Christian theologians can falsely set Christianity against Judaism in areas where they in reality share a genuine commonality.

All in all, the usefulness of Sobrino's Christology for the dialogue will be minimal. While his thought shares some of the positive features of liberation theology vis-à-vis the dialogue such as the incompleteness of history, the working out of the salvific process within history, and the constructive role of those outside the institutional Church in this process, he has so developed his understanding of Christian liberation in opposition to the Judaism of Jesus' day that only a fundamental reworking could alter this evaluation. His thought must be placed in the same camp as that of Pannenberg's: totally unacceptable in its present form because the positive meaning of each Christology is inextricably tied to the devaluation of Judaism. Despite the soundness of some of their major theses, both need to remold their Christology on the basis of a much more thorough and real understanding of the Judaism of Jesus' day and how he related to it.

While Sobrino's emphasis on Jesus' Abba experience and some of his other points relative to the meaning of Jesus' message about God could well prove useful for contemporary Christological construction, they remain problematical so long as they remain mired in his theological anti-

Judaism. Williamson's concluding remarks about Sobrino summarize the situation very well:

> Sobrino's whole project of a Christology for liberation theology is jeopardized critically by his way of approaching the historical Jesus. A liberation Christology that cuts itself off from *the* liberating event of the Bible, the Exodus of a people from oppression, from real slavery to real freedom is self-defeating. . . . What was proclaimed in the days of Moses has been also said to us Gentiles: namely, that evil, oppression, torture and death are real, all too real, but that they are not the last reality. The last reality is always God's new beginning, God's new initiative, the freedom, life, liberation, and righteousness that come from the gentle workings of a good not our own, a good redemptive of all people, even of those who resist God's new beginnings. Christianity will become a force for liberation when it rediscovers the connection between Easter and Exodus.[115]

The most recent major Christology work from the Latin American perspective to appear on the international scene is Leonardo Boff's *Jesus Christ Liberator*.[116] Boff's approach parallels that of Sobrino's in many respects relative to the Jewish question. While he acknowledges some positive aspects in the tradition of the Hebrew Scriptures which he says brought God into history, and while he admires the eternal optimism of the Jewish apocalyptic vision, his interpretation of Jesus' liberating spirit rests almost entirely on a rejection of the Judaism of Jesus' day. Like Sobrino he totally ignores the liberating dimensions of the Exodus covenantal tradition. Christ's preaching differed entirely from the Messianic expectations common to Judaism. Christ never fed the nationalism of the Jews nor did he strike out in rebellion against the Roman authorities. He likewise never alluded to the restoration of the Davidic king.

Boff plays down the historical discussions about the various titles attributed to Jesus (i.e., Son of God, Son of Man, Lord, etc.). They are not important in themselves. They all point in an incomplete way to a deeper and more pervasive reality—the liberation of the human community experience through the preaching and ministry of Jesus. This ministry and preaching postulated a new image of God and a new approach to God. Here Boff is on the same path as Sobrino. "God is no longer the old God of the Torah," he insists, but rather "a God of infinite Goodness, even to the ungrateful and the wicked. He draws near in grace, going far beyond anything prescribed or ordained by the law."[117]

For Boff, God is to be viewed primarily in terms of the future, in terms of the Kingdom that is being established. This Kingdom will mark a complete liberation from the evil mechanisms of past history and provide a fullness of life without parallel. Liberative praxis rather than cultic worship, prayers and strict religious observance constitute the surest path to the God revealed in Jesus Christ. Thus Christology for Boff is in many ways primarily a statement about the nature of God and his relationship to the human community. Motivated by the new vision of God, Jesus broke down all previous barriers among people. He spoke in behalf of a new solidarity above and beyond class differences. As Boff sees it, Jesus altered the center of gravity regarding the criteria for salvation. He subjected the Torah and the dogmatism of the Old Testament to the criterion of love, this "liberating human practice from necrophilic structures."[118]

Boff repeats Sobrino's contention that Jesus was condemned as a blasphemer, for he presented a God who was different from the God of the status quo. Though executed by the imperial authorities as a guerrilla fighter, his real crime was his opposition to the entrenched religious leadership of the time. In imitation of Sobrino, Boff seems to equate the leadership fundamentally with the Pharisees though he does not spend as much time denouncing them as the former.

Boff stresses that the Christological vision inherent in the New Testament provides us with an understanding of what is meant by the full humanization of people. While he does not highlight Jesus' Abba experience quite as much as Sobrino, his thesis about the ultimate implications of the Christ event is much the same. He also joins Sobrino in maintaining that all religions have salvific elements, with the implication that Christic structures are not the exclusive preserve of the institutional Church. If anything, he comes out more strongly and decisively on this matter than Sobrino.

There is not much by way of evaluation of Boff's Christology that has not been said with regard to Sobrino. Perhaps the tone of Boff's work overall is a little less severe toward the supposed shallowness of the Judaism of Jesus' day. But Boff joins Sobrino in trying to articulate the liberating experience of Jesus' message over against Judaism instead of linking it to the Exodus event as Gutierrez and Bonino do. Thus much of the criticism directed above at Sobrino applies with equal vigor to Boff's Christology. While it contains many notions that could be utilized in a reformulated Christology in the dialogue, the basis for its outlook would need to undergo a major shift of focus before it would deserve to be imported into a dialogue setting.

Concluding Observations

This cursory look at how several key figures in contemporary systematic theology relate their Christological ideas to Judaism clearly shows that many of the long-standing stereotypes remain in force. A few of the continental writers have begun to seriously question these stereotypes, particularly as a result of the Holocaust experience, but their attempts are still far behind the type of thorough rethinking found among the scholars whose views we examined in the previous chapter. This is to admit that the theological reflection that has taken place within the dialogue has yet to penetrate the Christian theological mainstream in any significant way. Among the Latin American liberationists there has been even less impact than among the Europeans. Several of the former have in fact only reinvigorated the long-standing stereotypes of Judaism by trying to define the freedom message of the Gospels in direct opposition to the imagined oppression of the Jewish Torah system.

Thus while there have been some breakthroughs among major Christian systematicians on the Jewish question, the general conclusion for the moment must still be that Christology continues to suffer from a deep anti-Judaic malady. Yet it would be wrong to assume an entirely pessimistic posture. There remains the hope that theologians like Moltmann and Küng, with their evident general sensitivity on the Jewish question, will finally begin to integrate this sensitivity more profoundly into their Christological construction. Also the universal emphasis among the theologians we have examined on the fact that the Kingdom of God must be seen as a future rather than a present reality breaks down one of the most pervasive distortions of Judaism in the Christological area, even among those theologians who have not specifically alluded to this point in their own writings. History has not yet come to an end as a result of the Christ event, as much of traditional Christian theology had claimed for so long a time. This assertion, gradually becoming a cardinal principle of contemporary Christology, will of necessity force Christian theologians to rethink the meaning of Judaism when formulating their Christological positions.

The Continental theologians have also more or less agreed upon the fact that Jesus can no longer be explained simply as the one who fulfilled the Messianic prophecies of the Hebrew Scriptures. This represents another breakthrough with positive ramifications for the discussion of Christology in a dialogue setting.

One inescapable conclusion from the study of the Continental and liberation theologians is that they all seriously lack a proper understanding of the Second Temple period in Judaism. If the scholarship on this period being undertaken increasingly by Christian and Jewish scholars begins to filter into the realm of systematics, then we may see how some of the Christological interpretations put forth by the contemporary authors are in fact but a reflection of the more progressive trends in the Judaism of Jesus' day. Thus, there would no longer be the temptation to articulate the meaning of the Christ experience in terms of Jewish rejection. Coupled with the heightened appreciation of the Exodus event introduced into Christology by Gutierrez and Bonino, the way would finally be opened for the development of a Christology that would positively incorporate Jewish values into its expression. That day, however, still lies ahead. Thus far, the major systematicians have only touched the outer fringes in dealing with the Jewish question in Christology. A genuine breakthrough continues to elude us. The subsequent chapter will try to show a path that may eventually lead out of this impasse.

4
Jesus' Teaching: Its Links with and Separation from Pharisaic Judaism

From the discussions in the preceding chapters it is obvious that this author feels that none of the proposed theological models for stating the Christian-Jewish relationship now in existence meet the full test of adequacy. This chapter will attempt to offer another model. While incorporating important insights from several of the scholars discussed previously, the constructive proposal to be presented here does not merely duplicate any of the previously formulated models. It has a definite uniqueness. Having said that, however, it likewise needs to be admitted that it is offered as a working proposal still in search of further clarification and modification. There are dimensions of this model that require further reflection and elaboration, but hopefully it will set the basic directions for further theological thinking in Christianity about the link between Church and Synagogue.

Pharisaism: Key to Christological Understanding

A common critique of the theological positions examined in the previous two chapters was that they lacked a sufficient acquaintance with the dynamism inherent in Second Temple Judaism; hence the supposition that any constructive model for the Jewish-Christian relationship must delve rather deeply into this period. Very frequently this era in Judaism, the so-called intertestamental period, has been characterized as one of great sterility, a time when the people had lost contact with the spirituality and traditions of the Jewish past. This supposed emptiness in Judaism, frequently referred to as "legalism," was then simplistically contrasted with the love and freedom central to the Gospel message. We have seen remnants of this point of view in Pannenberg, but especially in Sobrino and Boff. Jesus is there portrayed as coming on the scene to fill the spiritual void resulting from the religious emasculation of Judaism.

As an increasing number of scholars in recent years, both Christian and Jewish, have looked anew at the Second Temple period, a different picture has begun to emerge. Carl G. Howe, for example, has written that the period between the Old and the New Testaments was

> ... most active politically, intellectually, and spiritually. ... It was an active, creative era both in the one world of political struggles and in the fragmented world of man's inner life. ... When Jesus appeared, the world was vastly different from the world Ezra knew. Much happened in those four centuries, and one must understand these happenings if he wishes to comprehend the meaning of the New Testament.[119]

One of the most profound developments within this Second Temple period was the emergence of the Pharisaic movement. The ordinary Christian picture of the Pharisees is that of the arch-enemies of Jesus, the whited-sepulchres of Matthew's Gospel, a group which stood in total contradiction to the basic thrust of Jesus' message. Beginning with the pioneering work of the Unitarian scholar R. Travers Herford published in his volume *The Aim and Method of Pharisaism,*[120] there has been a steady stream of literature on the Pharisaic movement. Louis Finkelstein,[121] Asher Finkel[122] and Michael Cook[123] on the Jewish side and J. Massingberd Ford,[124] Rosemary Ruether,[125] Frederick Grant,[126] William E. Phipps,[127] and now Clemens Thoma[128] on the Christian side have all addressed themselves to the issue in a way that shatters the usual stereotypes of the Pharisees. The most extensive new research on the Pharisaic movement has been undertaken by Ellis Rivkin[129] and Jacob Neusner.[130] There are many points of agreement in their analyses, but profound differences also have surfaced. In part, this is due to their distinctive methodological orientations, Rivkin working as a professional historian and Neusner attempting to use scientific tools from biblical scholarship to interpret the Pharisaic documents. Another problem is that the materials on early Pharisaism are to be found only in volumes compiled well after the period of initial Pharisaic development. Hence it proves a difficult task at times to determine whether the ideas attributed in the existing texts to early Pharisaism really go back to that era or are in fact a reverse projection of much later outlooks. Yet, while many questions remain about the precise nature of the Pharisees, we now have a reasonably good skeleton of their fundamental élan.

The origins of the Pharisaic movement are clouded in uncertainty. Without doubt the birth of Pharisaism was gradual. When the historian Josephus, himself a loyal follower of the Pharisees, transcribed the history of the Jews in his *Antiquities* he was unable to uncover any sources explaining their origins and early development. They simply appear without warning in his narrative of the Hasmonean Revolt.[131] But whatever their origins, they had clearly established themselves by the end of the Maccabean period as a force bringing a quiet, yet far-reaching, revolution to the Jewish people, a revolution that has influenced the face of Judaism up into our own time. Despite their revolutionary goals, however, the Pharisees did not look upon themselves as a totally new phenomenon. As Rivkin puts it:

> They [the Pharisees] did not think they were carrying out a revolution, but a restoration. They did not consider themselves to be a ruling class, but one whose founder was Moses himself. They did not see themselves as the creators of the oral law but as its transmitters. They did not look upon the institutions that they brought into being as innovations nor their radical new concepts as novel. They viewed themselves as the champions of the eternal twofold law, revealed at Sinai, transmitted through the ages by leaders like themselves, and sustained by the powerful institutions embodying their authority as a class, the *Beth Din Ha-Gadol.* And even when they introduced new legislation, they believed that they were carrying out a traditional function, following in the footsteps of their authoritative predecessors, Moses, Joshua, the Elders and the Prophets.[132]

As the Pharisees grew in numbers and influence, and as the situation of the Jewish people deteriorated with the Roman conquest of Palestine that followed the short-lived experience of independence inaugurated by the Maccabean succession, the movement came up against the fundamental question of future Jewish survival. The Pharisees concluded that this issue had to be resolved in the context of Jewish tradition, but with an openness to the contemporary situation. Survival had to be meaningful for the people, not merely continued physical existence, and the pillars of meaning for the Pharisees were the Exodus covenant given to Moses and the teachings of the prophets.

The Pharisees continued the understanding of the Exodus covenant that had emerged with the prophets and the Deuteronomic reform. Basic to this interpretation of the covenant was the sense that the Sinai event had brought about an historic transformation in the human person's understanding of the term "religion." Prior to the Sinai experience "religion" was generally equated with cult or ritual. Worship was considered to be the highest religious expression of which the human being was capable. The terms of the Exodus covenant, however, had rendered this simplistic interpretation of religion obsolete. The necessity of worship was never at issue. The dialogue between Moses and Yahweh includes complex details for offering sacrifice. Yet, upon careful examination of the relevant passages in the Book of Exodus,[133] it becomes evident that the ritual prescriptions are not included in the covenant proper. Instead, the bulk of the legislation pertains to areas of justice and mercy rather than cult. What in fact had occurred through the Sinaitic theology was the expansion of the term "religion" to include social responsibility as an integral, inescapable part of its definition. Set within the context of the history of developing religious consciousness, this expanded Exodus notion of religion represented a crucial breakthrough. Any future attempt to separate concern for justice and mercy from worship would be tantamount to idolatry. This was the most unique and the most crucial realization resulting from the biblical theology of the covenant, but it is not meant to imply that worship was de-emphasized. Cult continued to play a vital role in the biblical understanding of religion. Its function, however, now was to complement and reinforce social responsibility in a more comprehensive notion of religion rather than to serve as the dominant component in religious expression, as had been the case up till then.

Coupled with this new understanding of religion was the sense of peoplehood and mission. The reign or Kingdom of God would not appear in its fullness until the day that justice and mercy dominated the social milieu. And this day of the Lord would come about only if and when people began working together to weave the ideals of justice and mercy into the fabric of human society, and thereby transforming it. The Exodus covenant reaffirmed the notion of the human person as co-creator, so forcefully articulated in the theology of Genesis.[134]

Anyone with even the barest knowledge of biblical history must be aware that the ideals of the Exodus covenant did not attain full expression in Jewish society during the biblical period. Prophets appeared on the scene time and time again to warn the people that they faced suffering and destruction if they failed to take seriously the obligations of the Exodus covenant. Though at times the prophets were concerned about the worship of idols, their major preoccupation always revolved around the areas of justice and mercy. They were not anti-liturgical per se, but they were deeply concerned about keeping alive the new vision of religion that the

Sinaitic theology had unlocked. They saw the people falling back into the older, pre-Exodus notion of religion in which worship was seen as the pre-eminent religious duty of the human person, and they tried to put a halt to this dangerously regressive trend. Their success was minimal at best, as both the northern and southern kingdoms of the Jewish people eventually fell into the hands of foreign conquerors. The prophets are crystal-clear about the cause of this downfall. "You have failed in justice and mercy," they tell the people over and over again.

After the northern kingdom had been captured and the southern kingdom stood on the brink of a similar disaster, King Josiah initiated yet another attempt to bring Jewish society into line with the social obligations inherent in the Exodus covenant. He, too, failed in this attempt, though the Deuteronomic reform he set into motion was to have a profound impact on later Jewish society and the early Christian Church. What Josiah began to perceive was that the ideals of the Exodus covenant would never materialize, short of some basic changes in the very structures and patterns of Jewish life.

This was the Sinaitic-Prophetic-Deuteronomic milieu in which Phari-saism was born and grew to maturity. The leaders of the movement looked back and reflected on Israel's past experiences and traditions in the light of the challenges facing Judaism in their own day. The Pharisees recognized and advanced the unique religious insights of the Exodus covenant, and they certainly exhibited a deep reverence for the contributions of the prophets. Still, they also detected a fatal flaw in the prophetic vision set forth in the Exodus theology. As the Pharisees evaluated the situation, the prophets had tended to restrict themselves to generalized warnings that spoke directly to the conscience of the people Israel. Such warnings, however, were shown to be insufficient by the course of events. Appeals for a transformation of personal moral conduct were simply not enough. They had not been able to prevent the pain and humiliation of the exilic punishment. Something more was needed. And the Pharisees sensed that Josiah was probably on the right track in his attempt to introduce structural reform alongside personal transformation.

The Pharisees quite correctly perceived that during the many centuries that had passed since the expanded notion of religion had first surfaced in human consciousness, little had been done to alter the religious structures of Jewish society. Structurally, cult continued to remain the principal religious expression of the human community, with the priest as the central religious figure and the temple as the chief religious institution. In fact this pattern had become even more entrenched in the period following the end of the Persian captivity and the re-establishment of the Jewish community around the Temple in Jerusalem.

When Ezra and his Jewish comrades grappled with the reasons for the pain and suffering endured by the people Israel during the exile, and how its recurrence might be avoided, they concluded that the only certain approach was a re-emphasis on cult. Hence the Temple was rebuilt in Jerusalem, the ritualistic laws were codified with great precision and thoroughness, and the Temple priests assumed the political-religious leadership of the people.

The Pharisees, however, became convinced that Ezra's reforms were not the route to take on a permanent basis, and that a different answer was called for. The Jewish people after all were once more under foreign domination—this time Roman. Their morale had sunk to a very low point and they were confronted with extinction as a result of both physical force and the lure of assimilation. The priesthood, especially in Jerusalem, had become largely corrupt, often selling out the best interests of the Jewish community at large for personal favors from the imperial authorities.

Such a situation left the Pharisees with little doubt that the only revolution that could save the people was not the armed revolution espoused by the Zealot movement but a fundamental change in the structures of Jewish society, in line with the expanded notion of religion expressed in the theological outlook of the Exodus covenant.[135] Four major changes were introduced into Jewish life by the Pharisees. They were (1) the new emphasis on the oral Torah, (2) the development of the rabbinate, (3) the emergence of the Synagogue as the central religious institution of Judaism, and (4) the table-fellowship in the home as a symbol of the power of the people.

The Pharisees and the Oral Torah

The Pharisees argued that the written Torah (basically the Pentateuch) had become more or less petrified. They rejected the claims of the Sadducees (the priestly party) that interpretation of the written Torah was the exclusive prerogative of the priestly class. Against this claim they introduced the novel concept of renewing a tradition rooted in group life. It was their contention that this tradition which they called *oral Torah* was just as authoritative as the written Torah. It too originated in the revelation of Sinai. As the Jewish scholar Stuart Rosenberg puts it:

> There [Sinai] the word of God—both the written Torah and its oral interpretations—was given by Moses to the whole people, not to any

special religious order, group of believers, or priestly leaders. The oral
Law is transmitted by the people from generation to generation, and it
grows as interpretations in the light of new problems are added to it.
Out of the hands of the priests, the rabbis took a fixed and unyielding
tradition that had become congealed in words and cultic practice, and
gave it over to the whole people. What is more . . . they ordained that all
who would study and master that tradition might teach it, expound it,
and ultimately even amplify it.[136]

The Pharisaic rabbis were convinced that all the traditional six hundred and thirteen commandments of the Hebrew Bible had to be carefully
restudied from the viewpoint of human need and the specific situation of
the day. The priestly tradition had looked upon the commandments
primarily in a cultic framework—they were means of sanctifying God. The
Pharisees felt that these commandments had to offer opportunities for the
sanctification of human life as well. The Pharisaic approach reshaped
prophetism and gave its lofty, humane concerns a concrete order and
structure. Every commonplace, daily human action could become sacred if
it were seen, as the rabbis intended it should, as an act of worship. The
loving deed, the "mitzvah," assumed an importance in many ways far
greater than the Temple cult. This new perspective opened the way for a
Jewish life-style that could continue to grow long after the destruction of
the Jerusalem Temple.

The Pharisaic rabbis developed what Rosenberg has called "rituals of
interpersonal behavior."[137] The commandments of the written Torah were
quite specific and detailed with respect to sacrificial laws and priestly
regulations. But what precisely did the Torah command when it said
"Honor your father and your mother," or "Love your neighbor as your-
self," or "Remember that you were once slaves in the land of Egypt"?
Questions such as these were a major concern of the Pharisees, and the
answers they provided to these questions turned oral Torah into something
far greater than extraneous commentary. Through the use of the oral
Torah process, the Pharisees deepened, humanized and universalized the
older traditions. As the priests had been concerned with the codification of
the cultic legislation, so the Pharisees concentrated their efforts on the
"codification" of love, loyalty and human compassion, with the expressed
goal of making them inescapable religious duties incumbent upon each and
every member of the people Israel.

How must a person love his/her neighbor? What are the ways in
which one must show respect for parents? What does freedom from
slavery mean in the concrete? The Pharisaic rabbis answered such ques-

tions by giving new meaning to the commandments found in the Penta-teuch. Propositions that had been very general in orientation were now spelled out as specific religious and moral duties to be lived out by all the members of the Jewish community. Hospitality to travelers, visiting the sick of all religious groups, dowering the indigent bride, universal educa-tion for all males, attending the dead to the grave and helping to bring peace to those for whom it was absent had never been clearly set forth as religious obligations in the Hebrew Scriptures, though they were implied in its spirit. The rabbis fashioned these concerns into new commandments, or "mitzvot," thus making communion with God possible at any given time or place, with or without the Temple, the priesthood and the sacrifi-cial altar.

What is clear from this Pharisaic concern with the oral Torah is the necessity for religious persons committed to the ideals of the Exodus covenant to move beyond mere nominal generalizations to concrete pro-grams that would correct the injustices being perpetrated by existing social structures. The rabbis were convinced that religious men and women had to offer concrete and detailed plans for changing unjust practices in a society. Only thus could they truly fulfill their role as co-creators. Only thus would the Messianic Kingdom of peace and justice be brought closer to realization.

The Pharisees and the Rabbinate

The Pharisaic revolution was marked by the gradual emergence of a new religious figure in Judaism called the rabbi. He assumed neither the traditional role of prophet nor of priest. This new leadership role was seriously challenged and criticized by the priestly class, even though the rabbis never laid claim to the biblical prerogatives accorded the priests. The rabbinic role was a by-product of the new emphasis on the oral Torah in Pharisaic circles. The rabbi's task was conceived as one embracing a twofold function: interpreting Torah and, even more importantly, specify-ing its generalized commandments found in the Pentateuch and the proph-ets into concrete duties that would answer the needs of Jewish society in any given period of history.

The crucial aspect of the rabbinate needing to be understood clearly is that the rabbi was not a cultic figure. His role was one of instruction and interpretation, and if we examine the issues with which the rabbis dealt, we will find that most of them fell into the category of social responsibility.

What is especially significant here is that a non-cultic figure, whose

primary responsibility resided in the determination of specific solutions to
the social problems facing the Jewish society of the day, gradually replaced
the priest as the principal human symbol and representative of Jewish
faithfulness to Torah. While it might be argued that kingship in Israel was
an earlier instance of a non-cultic figure assuming the role of chief
religious representative of the Jewish people, the situation in that instance
was not as clear-cut as it was in the case of the Pharisaic rabbi. For the
first time the expanded Exodus notion of religion had clearly resulted in
someone other than a cultic figure becoming the widely accepted symbol
of God's presence among people. In the figure of the rabbi, the Exodus
understanding of social responsibility as an integral part of genuine religion received concrete, symbolic expression for the first time.

It should be made clear that the rabbis of this period did not fit some
of the common stereotypes found among Christians today. We tend to
conceive of the rabbi as a scholarly, academic type who pores over his
manuscripts while locked up in his study, rather immune to the everyday
happenings of the world. In actual fact, the rabbis in the Pharisaic
perspective had to combine their teaching and study of the Torah in the
synagogue with concrete acts of mercy and healing among their people.
The criteria for judging an authentic rabbi included more than just the
ability to develop sound interpretations of the written Torah and to
demonstrate skill in synagogal debate. The ultimate test of the validity and
correctness of his views came in the field. Did he show mercy? Did he heal
those who were sick? These were the primary standards, along with
intelligence, for the rabbinate laid down in the Talmud.

The Pharisees and the Synagogue

The third pertinent dimension of the Pharisaic revolution was the
development of the institution which eventually came to be known as the
synagogue. Pharisaic Judaism does not appear to have consciously created
the synagogue. Rivkin says that it "emerged spontaneously in the course of
the Pharisaic revolution; it was not deliberatively invented."[138] Once in
existence, however, it grew rapidly throughout Palestine and the cities of
the diaspora.

From its inception, the idea of the synagogue focused around the
congregation as community. The emphasis definitely was not placed on the
synagogue as a sacred place, as a votive shrine or as a magnificent public
building. There is an important role assigned to prayer in the overall
synagogue scheme. Some synagogues even included an adjoining square

for ritual slaughter. Yet, in contrast to the Temple, the synagogue did not serve primarily as a place for prayer and worship. As Rosenberg puts it, "The synagogue transcended the Temple in the lives of the people because it became more than a 'House of God'—it became the 'House of the People of God.' "[139]

It was at the synagogue that the Pharisaic rabbis explained to the people the concrete demands of the oral Torah, particularly those relating to social responsibility. In fact, homilies on contemporary demands of the Torah, on the need for the performance of "mitzvot," were built into the fabric of the religious service for the first time in the history of Jewish liturgy. Rosenberg is quite correct in insisting that these homilies were much more than mere pedagogical devices. Worship, the rabbis were insisting, must be linked to ethical service. Prayer and worship without moral commitment are insufficient for fulfilling the imperatives of the biblical tradition. For the first time the chief religious institution of Judaism, or of any major world religion for that matter, placed concern for social responsibility on a par with ritual worship. In the synagogue the covenantal ideal of Exodus had received full institutional expression for the very first time. In keeping with their awareness that mere prophetic appeals to conscience were relatively ineffective by themselves in producing the transformation of Jewish society that they considered to be a requirement of the Sinai experience, the Pharisees enacted a profound structural change in Judaism by gradually replacing the Temple with the synagogue.

The synagogue soon after its inception became the haven of the people of Israel, a place of communal assembly. Courts of law carried out their responsibilities within its walls, strangers to the community were welcomed into its hostel, the poor were invited there to receive alms, and community philanthropies were administered by its councils. In time these broad communal and humanitarian functions were so well integrated with the religious and educational program that the synagogue became the supreme focus of all Jewish life. And this unique institution created by the Pharisees was destined to serve, as the Protestant historian Albert Reville pointed out, as "the mother of the Christian Church and also of the Muslim mosque."[140]

The Pharisees and Table Fellowship

The Pharisaic stress on the significance of table fellowship and the strict laws with which the Pharisees surrounded its observance need to be fully understood. A superficial acquaintance with them could easily lead one to conclude that the movement was indeed legalistic in the extreme, much as its detractors have frequently claimed. In actual fact, though this emphasis could on occasion result in an overly exclusivist mentality, the primary motivation behind table fellowship was far deeper.

Jacob Neusner is the scholar who has most studied this dimension of the Pharisaic movement. He is correct in perceiving its central importance for the Pharisaic movement, even though he may be guilty of some disproportion in his viewpoint by so elevating its significance above all other Pharisaic concerns.

As Neusner sees it, the table fellowship idea was the way in which the Pharisees hoped to alter the power center in Jewish life. They saw no immediate gains in directly opposing the oppressive Roman regime. Instead they turned their attention, as we have already seen, to the reshaping of life within the Jewish community. The Pharisees were determined to focus on elevating the life of all of the people, at home and in the streets, to the command of the Torah: You shall be a kingdom of priests and a holy people. Such a community would conduct its affairs as if it were perpetually living in the Temple sanctuary at Jerusalem. To symbolize this, the complicated and rather inconvenient priestly laws formerly prescribed only for the members of the Temple priesthood were extended to apply to the life of each and every Jew in his or her home. This, it must be clearly stated, was not merely an effort to burden additional people, but the way selected by the Pharisees to dramatize the shift in power and focus away from the Jerusalem Temple. A new sense of equality had come to the fore. The Temple altar in Jerusalem could be replicated at every table in the household of Israel. The old, inherited elite system based on birthright that formed the heart of the Temple priesthood system in Judaism had been undercut. A genuine change in the locus of power and authority was taking place within the people Israel. A quiet but entirely far-reaching revolution was at hand. There was no longer any basis for maintaining a select class of people who, because they were born into priestly families, automatically held a distinct status in the eyes of God and were the only ones who could communicate with Adonai. Inevitably, such "spiritual" power led to a redistribution of political power within the Jewish community. As Neusner writes:

> The Pharisees held that even outside of the Temple, in one's own home,
> the laws of ritual purity were to be followed in the only circumstance in

which they might apply, namely at the table. Therefore, one must eat secular food (ordinary everyday meals) in a state of ritual purity as if one were a Temple priest. The Pharisees thus arrogated to themselves—and to all Jews equally—the status of the Temple priests, and performed actions restricted to priests on account of that status. The table of every Jew in his home was seen as being like the table of the Lord in the Jerusalem Temple. The commandment, "You shall be a kingdom of priests and a holy people," was taken literally: everyone is a priest, everyone stands in the same relationship to God, and everyone must keep the priestly laws. At this time, only the Pharisees held such a viewpoint, and eating unconsecrated food as if one were a Temple priest at the Lord's table thus was one of the two significations that a Jew was a Pharisee. . . .[141]

After the actual destruction of the Jerusalem Temple by the Romans in 70 CE, this Pharisaic emphasis on the all-pervasive presence of God in the home enabled the Jewish community to survive and prosper at a time when extreme demoralization could have brought about the virtual disintegration of the community. Yohanan ben Zakkai, one of the leaders of post-70 CE Pharisaism, proclaimed that sacrifices greater than those of the Temple must characterize the activities of the Jewish community. If a person wants to fulfill his/her responsibilities to the God of the covenant at a period when the Temple has vanished, the offering must be what Neusner calls "the gift of selfless compassion." The altar formerly in the Temple must be re-erected in the streets and the marketplaces of the world, just as the purity of the Jerusalem Temple had to be maintained in the streets and marketplaces of that city:

The kingdom of ritually pure priests, the holy people, living in the sacred land, must perceive its vocation: to offer itself as the perfect sacrifice to God, to renounce selfishness in favor of selfless love, to bring to the altar, which is the home and street, the gift of obedience to God, which is love of neighbor. The rite of ritual purity outwardly expresses the inner right; the priestly people in its holy place offers up itself. Psalmist and Prophet had said no less.[142]

We now have some idea of the specifics of the Pharisaic revolution within Judaism. But the picture of the movement would remain seriously deficient without some consideration of the underlying theological outlook that motivated this comprehensive alteration in the patterns of Jewish existence.

Theological Underpinnings for Pharisaism

Upon close examination of available sources we come to recognize that the power behind the Pharisaic revolution lay in a fundamentally new perception of the God-human person relationship. The Pharisees proclaimed that the God of revelation was the heavenly Father of each individual person. No longer was God viewed simply as the Father of the patriarchs, as the eternal parent of the people Israel. Each and every person now had the inherent right and dignity to address him directly as Father. A sense of a new intimacy between God and the human person was beginning to dawn. He had now become the Father of each and every person. Rivkin sums it up this way:

> When we ask ourselves the source of this generative power, we find it in the relationship the Pharisees established between the One God and the singular individual. The Father God cared about *you;* He was concerned about *you.* He watched over *you;* He loved *you;* and loved *you* so much that He wished *your* unique self to live forever. . . . The Heavenly Father was ever present. One could talk to Him, plead with Him, cry out to Him, pray to Him—person to Person, individual to Individual, heart to Heart, soul to Soul. It was the establishment of this personal relationship, an inner experience, that accounts for the manifest power of Pharisaism to live on. . . . *Internalization* is the only road to salvation.[143]

This new understanding of God's relationship to each person was so overwhelming for the Pharisees that they felt obliged to develop new names for God, relying on the older biblical terms only when directly citing the Scriptures. They referred to him as *Makom,* "the all present"; *Shekhinah,* "the divine presence"; *Ha-Kadosh Baruch Hu,* "The Holy One Blessed Be He"; *Mi She-Amar Ve-Hayah Olam,* "He who spoke and the world came into being"; *Abinu She-Bashamayim,* "Our Father who art in heaven"; and *Shemayim,* "heaven." There is little doubt that these changes in God-terminology reflect the importance which the Pharisees attached to their new perception of God and his relationship to creatures. A profound change in self-understanding was taking place on the deepest levels of human consciousness.

In his insightful approach to the meaning of human history, Teilhard de Chardin frequently emphasized the importance of what he termed the *drifts* in human history over the unchangeable rhythms. What he meant by this was that periodically in the course of history human consciousness moves in fundamentally new directions. The process alters significantly the understanding of human existence, but such drifts are most often quite slow and hence difficult to recognize.[144] One can legitimately argue that the Pharisaic revolution, leading into the ministry and self-consciousness of Jesus, constituted one such monumental *drift* in human history. It profoundly reshaped the way that people would view God, the human person and their interrelationship. That is why the stress on Jesus' Abba experience by Schillebeeckx and by some of the liberation theologians seems so much on the right track. We will return to the connection between Jesus and the Pharisees in a moment.

One consequential doctrine from the new Pharisaic insight into the God-human person relationship was the notion of resurrection from the dead. This was definitely an innovation in Jewish religious thought, one that brought the Pharisees into bitter conflict with the Sadducees who denied the concept of resurrection. An echo of this conflict surfaces in the pages of the New Testament.

For the Pharisees the notion of resurrection was a direct consequence of their perceived change in the God-human person relationship. The integrity and uniqueness of each individual were deemed so precious in the eyes of God that they would not be extinguished by death. Somehow the individual person would live on in a profound union with the Father-Creator, but a union that still allowed for eternal distinctiveness and separation. The God of the Pharisees was not the God conceived in some Eastern religions who wished to totally reabsorb his creatures into himself. The notion of resurrection constituted the Pharisees' ultimate statement about the utter dignity and uniqueness of each human person.

Jesus and the Pharisaic Revolution: The "Apparent" Hostility

To speak of Jesus and the Pharisees in the same breath appears almost blasphemous to one who only knows Pharisaism through the pages of the New Testament. For the overall picture of the movement in the Gospels is anything but complimentary. Hence a definite problem arises for any claim that Jesus was strongly influenced by Pharisaism. It is a problem that does not lend itself to a simple resolution. In part this is due to the difficulty of defining exactly the teachings both of Jesus himself (in contrast to the post-Easter church) and of the Pharisees of Jesus' period (about whom knowledge is dependent on considerably later source materials). Rabbi Michael Cook, in addressing the issue of the Jesus/Pharisee relationship, is extremely cautious as to the conclusions that might be drawn at this moment in scholarship because of the interpretive difficulties involved. In general he feels that it is easier to speak about the similarities between the respective teachings of Jesus and the Pharisees than to make authoritative statements about their differences.[145] Cook's warning about the pitfalls facing anyone wishing to confront the Jesus/Pharisee relationship needs to be continually borne in mind, even though he may overdraw them to some extent. Within this cautionary framework, nonetheless, some suggested explanations can be advanced.

The first is that put forward in the writings of James Parkes, where a contrast is drawn between the relationship of Jesus with the Pharisees as portrayed in the Gospels of Matthew and Mark.[146] In the former, the tone of the relationship is one of serious conflict and hostility. Mark, on the other hand, presents the relationship in a much more reserved and respectful fashion. Parkes points out that in Mark the break between Jesus and the Pharisees does not take place until Jesus allows his disciples to eat corn from the field on the sabbath and himself proceeds to heal a man on the sabbath, justifying his actions by appealing to what was in fact a Pharisaic principle—the sabbath was made for man, not man for the sabbath.[147]
Prior to this encounter Mark portrays Jesus and the Pharisees as having a cool but interested approach to one other. The episode that changes all that in Mark is to be understood, says Parkes, within the complex political and social setting of the time in which the very survival of the Jewish people was threatened by persecution and assimilation.

Observance of the sabbath became for the Pharisees the principal vehicle for preserving Jewish communal identity and the vocation of the people Israel. Jesus, not unaware of the problem of Jewish identity (reminding the Hellenist Jews, who favored assimilation, that he had come to advance Torah, not to destroy it), still decided to emphasize the uncompromising dignity of each individual person. The conflict between Jesus and the Pharisees is thus for Parkes one of the rights of the community over against the rights of the individual person. Both Jesus and the Pharisees were correct. They simply decided to take their fundamental stands on different but equally important aspects of the total human situation. Neither told us how to resolve the fundamental problem at hand: How does one combine in a just manner the rights of the individual with the legitimate demands of the community, especially in a crisis situation such as prevailed in this period? This viewpoint on the conflict question would then see the much more antagonistic material in Matthew's Gospel as a later addition which reflects the hostilities between the Church and Synagogue after Jesus' death more than the actual relationship he had with the Pharisees during his own lifetime.

The second projected explanation of the hostility is based on sections of the Talmud which list seven types of people who call themselves Pharisees. This approach has been developed in the writings of David Flusser.[148] Five of these groups are described in a negative fashion. Even among the two "positive" types—the Pharisees of awe (or veteran Pharisees) and the Pharisees of love—there were substantial disagreements. The Gospel condemnations of the Pharisees, based on this information, would not need to assume the status of global denunciations. Instead they were most likely directed against certain subgroups within the movement who did not measure up to the religious ideals which the Pharisees of love considered crucial to the Pharisaic spirit. This spirit of Pharisaic self-criticism is also strongly emphasized by Clemens Thoma, as was noted in Chapter 2. The explanation has the advantage of requiring no inclusion of later material into the Gospel texts.

An additional support for this explanation would come from an understanding of the requisites of both Aramaic and Greek grammar. In each language the definite article must accompany the use of a proper name like Pharisee. In these languages, however, there is not necessarily the same "totality" connotation implied by the employment of the definite article as in English. In other words, it would be quite proper to translate "the Pharisees" in English as "some of the Pharisees," thereby reducing the force of the supposed Pharisaic opposition to Jesus.

Michael Cook is quite skeptical about the usefulness of this second approach.[149] In part the reason is the problem of determining whether the condemnation of the five groups of Pharisees mentioned in the Talmud really applies to the period of Jesus' ministry. He is of the opinion that the rebuke may refer to groups existing only in the period after Jesus. It is also unclear, he insists, based on the research of Ellis Rivkin, whether the "perushim" referred to in a negative fashion really were a part of the Pharisaic movement.[150] Yet Rivkin's research would in fact appear to strengthen at least the general argumentation of this second approach to the conflict, namely, that the supposed opposition is not as easy to understand as a literal reading of the Gospels would suggest. Rivkin has found that the term "Pharisee" was regarded negatively by the Pharisees themselves, who preferred to be known as scribes or the wise ones. The Sadducees used this term in a derogatory fashion relative to the movement, implying that they were "heretics." The members of the movement in turn could have employed a term used to downgrade them against those whom they considered the enemies of authentic Pharisaism as a way of heaping scorn upon them. In other words, in this perspective the denunciations of "the Pharisees" by Jesus may in fact be directed against people whom he and other "love Pharisees" considered destructive for the fulfillment of the new religious vision developed during the Second Temple period. It is not unknown in intergroup relations for a unit under attack to use names hurled at it against its own opponents. Certainly "the Pharisees" were under attack from the Sadducean/priestly elite.

Cook would prefer a third approach to dealing with the apparent Gospel conflict between Jesus and the Pharisees. This approach would stress the evident similarities of many of Jesus' key teachings with central tenets of Pharisaism, particularly the version espoused by Hillel. In so doing any simplistic theory of inherent opposition would automatically lose its credibility, even though there may exist no cogent explanation as yet why the Gospels seem to depict such opposition. The Shemah and the Golden Rule would be two concrete illustrations of commonality between the teachings of Jesus and the Pharisees. These parallels, says Cook, certainly tend to "temper the portrayal of a total overagainstness in the Gospels (relative to Pharisaism)."[151] David Flusser has also stressed some of the very same connections in his writings.[152]

It should be clear from the above discussion that an answer to Jesus' precise relationship to the Pharisaic movement remains rather tentative. What we can say, however, is that the widespread stereotyping of Pharasaic utter opposition to Jesus is simplistic in the extreme. Whatever their differences, Jesus and the Pharisees seemed to agree on many central principles for religious living. Hence it would not be wrong in my view to consider Jesus as a part of the general Pharisaic movement, even though in many areas he held a distinctive viewpoint. While eclecticism is frequently the easy way out of a serious scholarly disagreement, in this situation it is probably the correct route to take. That is, the explanation for the apparent Gospel conflict between Jesus and the Pharisees can be found only by taking all three approaches into consideration.

Pharisaic Influences on Jesus

As we carefully examine the ministry of Jesus, certain parallels between him and the Pharisaic movement become evident. On any number of occasions he is seen in the process of teaching the oral Torah, reinterpreting the Hebrew Scriptures in a manner more in line with the social setting in which he found himself. His general ministerial stress with its emphasis on teaching and healing without question falls into the general pattern set for the authentic rabbi. While he himself gives no clear indication of the type of "institutional" arrangements he would have his disciples make after his death, the example of the early Jerusalem church, which we can presume to reflect in at least a general way the teachings of Jesus, shows great similarities to the synagogue model advocated by the Pharisees. He likewise appears to have participated in Pharisaic-type fellowship meals, instituting the Christian Eucharist at the final one he attended.

In the area of doctrine the resemblances continue. Emphasis on love, on the Shemah, on the themes summarized in the Beatitudes and on the Resurrection indicate the presence of a strong Pharisaic spirit in the life of Jesus. In particular Jesus' stress on his intimate link with the Father picks up on a central feature of Pharisaic thought. Granted that Jesus' personal sense of identification with the Father, as Clemens Thoma insists, went far beyond the degree of linkage between humanity and divinity that the Pharisees were willing to admit. Yet this sense of God-human person intimacy is not totally new and unique with Jesus, as is usually believed by Christians. It represents an extension, albeit one of quantum proportions, of the new consciousness of the God-human person relationship experienced by the Pharisees. That is why I feel that the Christology of Schillebeeckx and of those liberation theologians who focus on Jesus' Abba experience has the possibility of being reworked in a way that would establish deep links with Judaism. It is unfortunate, however, that Schillebeeckx and the liberationists are totally unaware of such links. This ignorance nonetheless does not invalidate the potential in their thought for a constructive contribution to the dialogue in the Christological area.

Jesus and Pharisaic Liberation

As indicated in the previous chapter, two of the best known liberation theologians, Gutierrez and Bonino, associate the mission of Jesus with the same divine liberating action present in the Sinai event. The difficulty from the standpoint of the dialogue is their implication that somehow Judaism lost all contact with the spirit of freedom evident in the Exodus from Egypt, it being rekindled only through the ministry of Jesus. It is true to say from my perspective that Jesus in fact did emphasize in his public life the same consciousness of freedom present in the Exodus, even if he did not make the connection explicit. But Gutierrez and Bonino are dead wrong in making this effort an isolated action of Jesus. The presence of God had to be liberated from certain oppressive structures which had developed in Jewish society of the period. Jesus was acutely aware of this, but this awareness was not restricted to him alone. Rather, it was a central goal of the overall Pharisaic revolution in which he shared.

The past several years have witnessed a virtual deluge of articles and books dealing with the question of Jesus as a revolutionary figure. Various claims pro and con have been made in this regard. As we look at this body of literature, at least three important trends seem to emerge.

The first school of thought—best represented in the writings of the late S. G. F. Brandon—maintains that the "meek" Jesus was a clever fabrication by the Gospel writers to avoid Roman persecution. In his *Jesus and the Zealots,*[153] Brandon asserts that Jesus, if not himself a Zealot, harbored strong Zealot sympathies. He was a political activist and a messianic revolutionary who, like the Zealots of his time, wanted freedom for Israel.

Though Brandon is the one most responsible for publicizing this revolutionary image of Jesus in present-day popular consciousness, his viewpoint is not totally new. In 1929 already, Robert Eisler, an Austrian Jewish scholar, claimed that Jesus yielded, though somewhat reluctantly, to his followers' persuasion and assumed an active role in armed insurrection against the Romans—a move which led to his execution.[154] Eisler's thesis was expanded by an American scholar, Joel Carmichael, who argued in his *The Death of Jesus*[155] that Jesus in fact commanded an armed attack on the Temple compound, and in consequence thereof was eventually brought to trial on a charge of sedition. Carmichael concluded that the New Testament chroniclers tried to soften Jesus' militancy "by spiritualizing it out of reality."

The second major interpretation of Jesus' socio-political attitudes has been best articulated by Oscar Cullmann, especially in his *Jesus and the Revolutionaries.*[156] In briefer form, the same interpretation is presented by Robert Grant in his contribution to the excellent symposium "The Trial of Jesus in the Light of History."[157] This school of thought views Jesus as primarily a radical religious reformer who was not directly involved in political action but stressed the need for people to change their hearts. Cullmann grants that as a result of their conversion some of Jesus' followers may well have taken a direct political role, but he insists that Jesus himself refrained from such activity. At the same time he acknowledges the likelihood that Jesus was put to death by the Roman authorities as a Zealot. In other words, Cullmann makes it clear that while he does not rule out contemporary social action in the name of Jesus' Gospel, he rejects all attempts to transform Jesus himself into a "revolutionary" social reformer. Such attempts, he believes, contradict scriptural evidence.

The third school of thought is not totally different from the first in that it clearly affirms Jesus as a person interested in socio-political change in his day. Its principal disagreements with the Brandon school come in its firm conviction that the New Testament portrays Jesus as totally committed to non-violent change (hence anti-Zealot), that the Church must always maintain a distance and integrity apart from the secular sphere in working for social change, and that while a Christian is obligated by faith to try to improve the social conditions in which he or she lives, the reality of sin makes the chances of widespread success very slim indeed. The value of social protest in this line of thought lies principally in its witness to a higher religious reality which the usual oppressive structures of society tend to hide. A leading exponent of this perspective is John Howard Yoder whose volume *The Politics of Jesus*[158] represents the most developed form of his thinking in this regard.

Since in terms of the basic orientation to the question the Brandon-Yoder approaches represent a unity, we will concentrate on trying to shed some light on the Brandon-Cullmann controversy. I should emphasize, however, before leaving Yoder entirely that while I respect the witness of the non-violent approach to social change and feel that it has a definite place in the totality of the Church's mission, I do not believe that the New Testament data produces sufficient evidence for an absolute rejection of violence in the quest for justice. That question—violence/non-violence—will have to be settled in the light of present-day exigencies. I would also have serious problems with what I consider to be Yoder's overly pessimistic stance on the possibilities for constructive social change. In his mind, Christians can at the most hope to be prophets. I am convinced that we can truly be builders as well.

The present state of scholarship regarding Jesus' social views can perhaps best be described as one of polarization. All the views put forward thus far suffer from serious weaknesses. The Brandon position simply relies too heavily on the totally undocumented claim that the Gospel writers distorted the picture of Jesus for security reasons. Given the political climate of the day, it is conceivable that such distortion could have occurred, but "could have" is a far cry from "did." On its side, the Cullmann position takes an overly simplistic view of the political power situation in Jesus' time. Both schools of thought make false assumptions that greatly contribute to the current polarization on the question. The first assumption is the virtually unchallenged equation: revolutionary equals Zealot. The second identifies a revolutionary too closely with violence of the Zealot type, thereby erroneously making violence central to a revolutionary posture. The understanding of the Pharisaic movement presented above can greatly help us to arrive at a more accurate assessment of Jesus' political activities.

With Cullmann and Grant, I reject the Eisler-Brandon thesis as unproved and probably unprovable (since it is most unlikely that any new first-century documents will be discovered which would substantiate their claim that the evangelists "soft-pedaled" Jesus' revolutionary stance). I equally object to one component of the Cullmann-Grant approach: namely that, having correctly rejected the idea of Zealot connections for Jesus, they immediately move to the personal-conversion model in portraying his mission. Surely a leap such as this rudely disregards the complexity of political life in Roman-controlled Palestine. The Zealots were by no means the only political activists of the period. Denying that Jesus was a Zealot does not automatically rule out the possibility of his association with other, equally revolutionary, political movements. The Cullmann-Grant school must at least acknowledge the existence of these other movements and examine Jesus' possible relationship to them before coming down so strongly for the personal transformation model as the *sole* design of Jesus' ministry. Not that personal transformation did not form an important element in Jesus' teaching; the issue is: Did it include more than this?

Any thorough investigation of the question of Jesus and the revolutionaries must take into account the highly complex distribution of political power in Roman-controlled Palestine. The Romans always preferred to govern their colonies through local people. Inevitably, therefore, two levels of power were created: (1) ultimate Roman political authority, and (2) everyday governing power in the hands of indigenous collaborators with the Roman regime. Such a division of power and authority obtained in the Palestine of Jesus' day. The local group was composed of the ruling clique of the Jerusalem priesthood headed by the high priests Annas and Caiaphas. These men not only controlled the strictly religious activities of the Jewish community but also determined its political and social cast. That they were generally corrupt and interested chiefly in their own survival rather than in the welfare of the Jewish people is evident to anyone who has read the history of those times, whether written by ancients or moderns. During the period of Jesus' active ministry the power of this group was being seriously challenged by the Pharisees, as we have indicated above. The growing influence of the Pharisaic movement, combined with the Zealot threat, was exerting pressure upon the high priests from the Roman side as well. Pontius Pilate's presence in Jerusalem testifies to

Rome's increasing distrust of the ability of the Temple leadership to control the situation.

Such was the political picture in Palestine at the time of Jesus. The point to be stressed is that there were two levels of political authority—the ultimate Roman and the subordinate priestly. Both were under attack. The Zealots went directly after the Romans. Their approach was violent, they were heavily outnumbered, and, as is well known, they were eventually "liquidated" in a bloodbath. Apparently it was their belief that the Messiah would join them and lead them to victory, which motivated them to undertake violent battle in the face of staggering odds. The Pharisees, on the other hand, attacked the subordinate authority—the Temple priesthood. Their approach, less eschatological and less violent, was rooted in a new theological understanding of the God-human person relationship.

Whether out of pragmatism or idealism (probably both), the Pharisees rejected the Zealot call for violent political change. They did not think it possible to overthrow the Roman suzerainty; therefore, reluctantly, they tried to accommodate themselves to it. Unlike the Zealots, their eschatological hopes were not of the highly "imminent" variety. Thus they had little reason for rushing into direct confrontation with the overwhelming military might of the Roman armies. Moreover, they recognized that a change in the local political authority would probably bring about an alleviation of the hardships imposed upon the Jewish community by the self-serving priestly regime. To this must be added the pacifist strain in Pharisaism, evident in their toning down the importance of Hanukkah (the festival commemorating the military victory of the Maccabees) and, indeed, in the Beatitudes of the New Testament which are deeply imbued with the Pharisaic spirit. Given this orientation, the Pharisees would hardly consider people of the Zealot type who were slitting throats in the alleys of Jerusalem as forerunners of a new, humane society.

Rather than attacking the imperial authority, the Pharisees concentrated on ending the dominance of the corrupt priestly clique and the Temple system which sustained it. The creation of the rabbinate, the meal fellowship and the synagogue were in part intended to achieve this goal. Ultimately the Pharisees succeeded in transforming the structures of Jewish society and giving them a more "democratic" bent. Particularly after the destruction of the Temple at the hands of the Roman forces in 70 CE and the political/social system which grew up around it, the new Pharisaic institutions took a firm hold within Judaism.

The point to be emphasized, then, is that the Pharisees were political activists who successfully challenged the intermediate political authority of their day by creating new religio-political forms rather than by direct use of violence. It must be admitted, however, that the Pharisees never had to confront the issue of the violent overthrow of the establishment; the Romans took care of that. Nonetheless, it might have been possible for the Pharisees to effect a power change without resorting to violence, despite the complexity of the situation.

In any case, an understanding of the Pharisaic viewpoint provides an option other than the Zealot one for a claim that Jesus participated in political action. Having already indicated Jesus' participation in the Pharisaic movement, we can now place the New Testament much more squarely within the political struggles of the period and so begin to appreciate some of Jesus' teachings and actions in a political light.

What I am saying is that, properly situated within the context of its own time, the New Testament is not as non-political as some have made it out to be. When we cease erroneously equating a political-revolutionary with a Zealot, as the Brandon school proposes, and admit the existence of the Pharisaic challenge, we can discern concrete political overtones in Jesus' teachings and activities. The problem is not with the Gospel accounts but with later interpreters who forged a distinction between the political and the religious which did not obtain in Jesus' day and who consequently went on to overspiritualize his teachings. This trend is only now being reversed, with the liberation theologians leading the way. Once we link Jesus with the Pharisaic attempt to change the day-to-day government of the Jewish people, we can see how many of Jesus' political references are in fact preserved in the Gospel narratives as they have been handed down to us.

Let me deal with just two examples. In his own day, Jesus' statement about destroying the Temple and raising it up again in his own body in three days could not possibly have been interpreted as a purely religious assertion. It was only later that Christians, conditioned to the idea of the separation of religion and politics, could understand it as such. However, to the Jewish audience Jesus was addressing, the Temple was not merely a place of worship. To the common person, it represented a total religio-political system marked by oppression. Hence Jesus' statements constituted a direct threat to the entrenched power that governed Palestine in its everyday affairs. It was as much a political statement as a call to destroy the White House or City Hall would be today.

The second key episode is Jesus' invasion of the Temple to drive out the moneychangers. Traditionally this pericope has been interpreted as a protest against cultic impurity. Properly placed in the context of the day, however, Jesus' action is a direct challenge to the total Temple system, not just to its religious practices. Indeed, Annas and Caiaphas clearly saw it as a rebuke. The full significance of the expulsion of the moneychangers from the Temple precincts has not been grasped by most commentators, although that situation is slowly changing. The explanations generally given stress that the moneychangers were desecrating a holy place and Jesus wished to cleanse and purify it. While this may have been a part of Jesus' intent, to leave the commentary at this is to miss the full impact of Jesus' action.

In the Gospel narratives, as we have them, this event takes place just prior to Jesus' Passion and death. Though this incident may in fact have been part of a much earlier visit to Jerusalem by Jesus (and hence resulted in his notoriety, as the New Testament scholar Etienne Trocmé maintains),[159] its location within the *theology* of the Gospels transforms it into a kind of "culminating" passage. It serves as a terse yet powerful summation of everything Jesus had been teaching and doing for three years in his ministry. The question here is not that Jesus was against the type of worship practiced in the Temple, but that he recognized the severe limitations and dangers in the whole Temple system. This system placed sacrifice at the center of Jewish life and established the priests as the chief religious figures of Judaism. Missing was the concern with justice and mercy that for the Pharisees had to be coupled with worship in any genuine understanding of religion. The evils which the Temple system and the segment of the Jerusalem priesthood in control of the Temple were inflicting on the Jewish people at large only served to highlight the basic inadequacies of the Temple model.

Albert Nolan has emphasized this same general interpretation of the Temple incident in his volume *Jesus Before Christianity: The Gospel of Liberation.*[160] He correctly rejects the view that fundamentally the invasion had anything to do with the sacrificial rites and ceremonies which took place there. Jesus' concern, according to Nolan, "was not to gain power or to purify ritual. His concern was *the abuse of money and trade.*"[161] There is ample evidence outside the Gospels for the fact that the moneychangers took advantage of the demand for clean animals for sacrifice by charging exorbitant rates, with some of the excessive profits likely going to the priests. "Jesus was determined to do something about it," says Nolan. "His compassion for the poor and the oppressed overflowed once more into indignation and anger."[162]

The point not adequately made by Nolan in his analysis of this pericope is that Jesus' concern about the oppression of the poor by the moneychangers was not an isolated criticism of Temple activities but represented a basic protest against the Temple system itself. It was the whole style of worship and the exclusive status of the priests that made possible the concrete abuses in the selling of sacrificial animals. In Jesus' mind it was not enough just to stop them, the whole Temple system needed to be replaced.

The conclusion that needs to be drawn from the New Testament in its present form, then, is that Jesus was a political activist who directly challenged the political power of the Temple priesthood. We need not look to the discovery of pre-New Testament material to establish this fact; it is plain from the Gospels as they are, provided that we bring to bear a sufficiently sophisticated understanding of political power in Jesus' day and do not restrict political activism to the Zealots.

Given the above New Testament portrait of Jesus, is it proper to term him a "revolutionary"? The answer depends mainly on how we define the term. Certainly, as used today, the word is a meaningless political catch-all. In the debate about Jesus' political stance, as we have seen, one finds the false equation between revolution and violence. More relevant to the resolution of the question is the theological substrate of the Pharisaic movement described above. The new sense of intimacy between God and the human person that stood at the heart of Pharisaism undercut the intermediary/hereditary elite system which had determined much of the social and religious patterns in Judaism up till then. There no longer remained any justification for maintaining a select class of people who, because they were born into priestly families, automatically held a distinct status in the eyes of God. The table fellowship of the Pharisees was shared equally by all members of "the kingdom of priests." Inevitably such "spiritual" power led to political power. The change-over from the priestly form of leadership to the rabbinic model brought about by the Pharisaic revolution did away with the system of power acquired by inheritance rather than by merit and service. Alteration of power centers and the distribution of power, of course, lie at the core of genuine revolutionary change.

Two further aspects of Pharisaism must be considered in dealing with the issue of revolution. The first has to do with the need for institutional change. The Pharisees tried to concretize the ideals previously articulated by the major prophets of Judaism by replacing the principal religio-political institutions of Jewish society. If fundamental changes in social structures are crucial for genuine revolution, as I think they are, then the Pharisaic/Jesus effort qualifies as revolution.

Secondly, the Pharisees reinterpreted the demands of the written Torah through the process of oral Torah, as we have seen. The specific injunctions developed in the oral Torah had the concrete effect of reshuffling power in Jewish society in a more egalitarian manner. Political power is hard to come by when one is hungry or unable to protest unjust wages or working conditions. As the historian of revolution, Crane Brinton, has shown, lasting revolutions rarely come from the really destitute in society.

As we examine the Pharisaic movement and recognize Jesus' close connections with it, we can perceive truly revolutionary elements. Let me clarify this statement by defining "revolution." As I view it, revolution is the process whereby a segment of society experiences alienation from existing social structures. This alienation, if activated, leads to the creation of new social structures that bring about more equality. The key point to be made is that revolution does not lead solely to structural change but to a new awareness of basic human equality. This consciousness, in turn, alienates people from present structures that deny such equality. However the alienation does not result in despair or anarchy but in the replacement of defective institutions with some that better embody the new consciousness. In their perception of the God-human person relationship and the consequent creation of such institutions as the synagogue, the rabbinate and the fellowship meal, the Pharisees and Jesus certainly meet this definition of revolution.

How exactly to describe the "revolution" involved in the ministry of Jesus remains a terminological problem. Francis Fiorenza has made a suggestion which seems to have definite possibilities, since it stresses the change in the notion of God which, as we saw above, was so central for Pharisaism. While in basic sympathy with the liberation theologians, he feels that by placing the emphasis in the revolution wrought by Jesus primarily upon "emancipation" or "liberation," one fails to accentuate the solidarity that lies at its base. He writes:

> The expression "emancipatory solidarity" places together atonement and redemption, reconciliation and salvation. One cannot exist without the other. The basis of our redemption is God's presence in Jesus expressing his solidarity with us in and through Jesus. . . . But his solidarity was interwoven with an emancipatory praxis. He healed the sick, cast out demons, forgave sinners, and fed the hungry. . . . In his

actions, the kingdom that he proclaimed was already anticipated, for his actions were signs of the future kingdom. Yet he was killed for the emancipatory solidarity expressed in his preaching and deed. . . . This proclamation and life-praxis not only defines Jesus but equally important involves a radical change in the understanding of God. It defines God not as a symbol of transcendent sovereignty but as a symbol of "emancipatory solidarity."[163]

The attempts by Gutierrez and Bonino to link the liberation involved in the Exodus event with the freedom accorded in Jesus can be turned into a constitutive link between Judaism and Christianity. It is to be deeply regretted that they portray Jesus as having alone resuscitated the revolutionary spirit of the Exodus, rather than understanding him as part of a much wider movement in Judaism. It is also most unfortunate that other liberation theologians such as Boff and Sobrino totally ignore this connection. One does not have to set Jesus over against the totality of Judaism in his time to retain his revolutionary credentials. Hopefully, this realization will begin to filter into the liberationist interpretation of Jesus' ministry which has much to offer Christological reinterpretation in our day.

Was Jesus a Pharisee?

At this point it would be useful again to directly address the question of Jesus' precise relationship to the Pharisaic movement. Can he be considered a son of the movement? The answer seems to be affirmative even though on several key issues which we shall examine shortly he was without doubt his "own man." And in his symbolic invasion of the Temple precincts he probably went far beyond what Pharisaic prudence would have allowed. William Phipps observes that it is possible to detect in the Gospels Jesus' agreement with the succinct description of the Pharisees offered by the Jewish historian Josephus: "The Pharisees are a group of Jews who have the reputation of excelling the rest of their nation in the observance of religion."[164]

Phipps feels that given the evident agreements and disagreements between Jesus and the Pharisees he can best be described as "a Pharisee who engaged in intense interaction with other Pharisees."[165] This approach on the part of Jesus was not really so unusual since the Pharisees tolerated a considerable diversity of viewpoints within their own ranks. Thus Jesus' ministry must be seen as thoroughly rooted in the ethos of Pharisaism, even though Jesus himself went beyond the boundaries of the movement in many ways. There is no other Jewish movement of the day to which his thought is more closely related. Phipps puts it well in his concluding statement:

> Jesus was like the resourceful scribe whom he commended as being able to "bring out of his treasure what is new and what is old" (Mt. 13:52). On the one hand he rejected the view that "the older, the better" is as true for religion as for wine (Lk. 5:39). On the other hand he defended but few novel ideas that had not been accepted by at least some of the Pharisees. He, like his prophetic antecedents, carried on a lover's quarrel with the traditions of his people. Hence, to argue that Jesus could not have been a Pharisee because of his polemics against the Pharisees is no more plausible than to maintain that Jeremiah could not have been a patriot because he was a caustic critic of the prevailing conduct of the Judean people. Those two prophets regarded themselves as purifiers—as tearing down in order to rebuild the group from which they came—even though some of their leaders thought of them as traitors and wanted them liquidated.[166]

Having established the deep connections between Jesus and the Pharisaic movement, we can now turn to some of the differences that exist in order to open up what appear to be unique dimensions of his teaching. The word "appear" is carefully chosen, for it is important to respect at this point the cautions of Rabbi Cook because of the source problems involved. The following, however, seem to be important differences at this moment of scholarly inquiry. In the first place is the degree of intimacy involved in Jesus' Abba experience. No Pharisee of his day would have been willing to grant the possibility of so close a link between humanity and divinity. The consciousness of a profound tie was certainly present in Pharisaism, but notions of separation, of distance, remained firm and unbending in the mind of even the most liberal members of the movement.

The second difference has to do with Jesus' attempt to carry the Pharisaic notion of the basic dignity of each human person to its ultimate conclusion. While the Pharisees' notion of God's intimate link with every human being bestowed an inherent value on every life, they were also concerned about the realities of the socio-political context in which they lived. James Parkes has written extensively on this point. The Pharisees gradually began to look upon Jesus' independent stress on the worth of the individual as a potential threat to Jewish communal survival. They were concerned with the absorption of Judaism by Hellenism and thus insisted on erecting what they termed "a fence around the sabbath" as a safeguard against the destruction of the people Israel. Jesus, on the other hand, showed that he was prepared to ignore the fences about the sabbath—its basic observance was never at issue—and to justify his actions with the generalization that the sabbath was made for man and not man for the sabbath. Though this principle is in fact in line with fundamental Pharisaic teaching, it was judged by them too dangerous a stance for their time. The popularity of Jesus raised a threat to national loyalty to Torah which the provisions for strict sabbath observance were intended to aid and ensure.

Parkes says that it is essential to realize that in this conflict the Pharisees could no more have simply accepted Jesus' teaching than he could have given in to theirs. His healing of a man's diseased hand on the sabbath, for example, was not in itself the crucial issue. Rather it was done deliberately by Jesus "as an assertion of the primacy of each man as person."[167]

Yet Parkes insists that Jesus never attempted as far as we know to discuss with the Pharisees how to achieve a reconciliation between the needs of the individual person and the legitimate demands of the community. Parkes warns that such reconciliation cannot be achieved by reliance on any simple formula. Quoting William Temple who said: "Revelation is an event; its interpretation is our responsibility," Parkes says that Jesus never tried to bridge the gap between his own vision and the understandable Pharisaic concern for the preservation of the community:

> Within the divinely chosen community he proclaimed the divine concern with each man as person. It is for men to hold the two in a continuously destroyed and continuously recreated balance. Jesus did not attempt to resolve the tension for us. He challenged us only to recognize that it existed.[168]

Thus, while the Pharisees pushed the concept of each individual's worth a tremendous distance, Jesus stretched it to its final limits. But it needs to be remembered that he did this with full consciousness that the notion of community was already a strong part of the tradition of the people whom he was addressing. Maintaining the proper balance in the ongoing community/individual tension is a task he left for us. Too often, however, the Christian churches have overemphasized the individual dimension at the expense of the communal. Jesus was willing to push the dignity of the individual and its practical implications beyond the prevailing Pharisaic consensus. However, it is hard to imagine, given his deep immersion in the spirit of the people Israel, that he ever meant this emphasis to erode the strong communal orientation which marks the Hebrew Scriptures.

Another possible distinction between Jesus and the Pharisees concerns their respective attitudes toward the *am ha aretz,* the people of the land. Frequently Jesus is portrayed as the great champion of this rather poor group while the Pharisees supposedly looked upon them with great disdain. Without doubt it is possible to establish on the basis of New Testament data Jesus' persistent interest in the welfare of the *am ha aretz.* What is not so certain is the contention that this put him out of step with mainline Pharisaic thinking. The research undertaken by Ellis Rivkin and Michael Cook leads them to conclude, in Cook's words, that "the presumed antipathy between the Pharisees and the '*am ha aretz*' is . . . not easily demonstrable."[169]

Jacob Neusner does not deal with the problem directly in his writings. To the extent that he tries to revolve Pharisaic identity around the exclusive table fellowship meal, his research would lend some credence to the view that Jesus and the Pharisees differed significantly in their approach to this group. However, it is not altogether clear that Neusner wishes to make his table fellowship thrust of Pharisaism the movement's exclusive emphasis.

This is an area that definitely needs further research on the part of scholars. At the moment, all we can say is that there seems to be something in the contrast between Jesus and the Pharisees on this point, though all exaggeration of the difference must be studiously avoided. Jesus, in line with his deep commitment to stress the inviolable dignity of each human person, was more ready to welcome the *am ha aretz* into the company of his disciples and perhaps even into his table fellowship meals than was the case for the Pharisees.

A fourth distinction between Jesus and the Pharisees emerges from the research of Shmuel Safrai and David Flusser.[170] They explain that Jesus took a rather well-known rabbinic saying about a person's inability to serve two masters and subtly changed it. For both the rabbis and Jesus, the first master was God. They differed, however, on the primary source of opposition to divine discipleship. The Pharisaic rabbis insisted that it was "evil inclination" which probably had a sexual base. Jesus changed this, perhaps under Essene influence, to wealth (or mammon). Thus, for Jesus riches are the antithesis of authentic commitment to God. Riches tend to drive a person away from God because in the process of securing wealth one frequently has to act in a manner that disregards the basic dignity of men and women. Once again we see how central the affirmation of human beings in their basic personhood was to Jesus' proclamation of the Word and the Way.

David Flusser is also responsible for bringing to the surface another unique quality of Jesus' message. It has to do with his attitude toward one's enemy. Following through on his stress on the fundamental dignity inherent in each person, Jesus urged upon his followers a positive attitude of respect for even those who had wronged them. This, Flusser says, stands in contrast to Pharisaic teaching which only insisted that the person be free of hatred toward the enemy but never insisted in the same way on the need to show love toward him or her. Flusser writes:

> It is clear that Jesus' moral approach to God and man . . . is unique and incomparable. According to the teachings of Jesus you have to love the sinners, while according to Judaism you have not to hate the wicked. It is important to note that the positive love even toward the enemies is Jesus' personal message. We do not find this doctrine in the New Testament outside of the words of Jesus himself. . . . In Judaism hatred is practically forbidden. But love to the enemy is not prescribed.[171]

Here we have another instance where the dignity of the individual assumes a primacy for Jesus that takes him beyond Pharisaism. As on other issues, Jesus pushed a fundamental Pharisaic point of view to its outer limits.

Notice must also be taken of Clemens Thoma's assertion that Jesus preached the actual presence of the Kingdom of God in his activities and person in a way that alienated him from Pharisaism. While it was stressed in Chapter 2 that Thoma rejects any notion of the Kingdom being *fully* present in Jesus and posits the full reconciliation of God and the human community as a still future event, it was not *entirely* in the future, as the Pharisees seemed to imply. While care must be exercised in stating this difference lest we fall back into the old Messianic-fulfillment Christologies which Thoma has rightly rejected, there does seem to be some basis for differentiating the stances of Jesus and the Pharisees along these lines.

The final point of contrast that we will look at relates to the question of the forgiveness of sin. Despite their generally liberal interpretation of religion, the Pharisees continued to hold tenaciously to the traditional view that God alone had the power to forgive sins. Jesus claims this power for himself. This is of course less than surprising in view of his general consciousness of a special relationship with the Father. But he does more than this. He transfers this same power to his disciples. This is indeed a revolutionary move. It represents in the theological milieu of its day a powerful statement about the intimacy between humanity and divinity. God stands willing to share with the human community one of his most treasured prerogatives—the power to reconcile. While the Pharisees, as we have seen above, strongly emphasized the new intimacy between God and people of which they had become conscious, they were clearly unwilling to go this far in their concept of the sharing relationship. This action on the part of Jesus further adds to the dignity of the human person upon which his ministry so prominently turned.

5

Christological Development and the Uniqueness of Christianity

Having tried to highlight, albeit in capsule form, the apparent similarities and differences between Jesus and the Pharisaic movement, we need now to turn our attention to the shift toward Christology. As the early Church began to theologize about the significance of the ministry of Jesus, how was Judaism's role conceived? Rosemary Ruether has charged, for example, that anti-Judaism became Christology's "left hand."

The Movement towards Incarnational Christology

The development of the earliest New Testament Christologies is a difficult picture to reconstruct with certainty. Great scholarly discussions have been held on the subject. There has been considerable work done, for example, in trying to pinpoint the meaning of the various titles accorded to Jesus. Recently, however, the liberation theologians as well as such figures as Schillebeeckx and Küng have begun to play down the significance of the individual titles such as "Son of Man," "Son of David," etc. They would stress rather the underlying reality that all these titles were trying to express, though in a highly imperfect fashion. At the heart of this underlying reality is the notion of the Incarnation, the Word made flesh. As a result of Jesus' teaching and ministry and through contact with his person, the early Church reached a deeper understanding of the intimate link between humanity and divinity.

At this point, it may be well to say something about the Resurrection and its role in the notion of Christology. Traditionally the Resurrection has been central to the interpretation of Christology. On the other hand, as we saw in Chapter 2 a dialogue theologian such as A. Roy Eckardt feels that the Holocaust has made it imperative for the Church to abandon its proclamation in this regard. The Resurrection-notion has been responsible in his mind for a triumphalistic interpretation of Christology that has done immeasurable harm to the Church.

The above approach to the ministry and teaching of Jesus will necessitate some serious rethinking of the role that the notion of resurrection will occupy in a reconstructed Christology. This will result in large part from a better understanding of the origins of the concept in Pharisaic theology. As we have seen, the resurrection of the individual was for the Pharisees their final statement about the new dignity of the individual person that they had uncovered in their reflections. It made the point that God so loved and respected each man and woman, that each person had such uniqueness and worth in his sight, that all would continue to live on forever in a separate, but not totally separated, existence. However, the notion of resurrection was for the Pharisees in a sense a derivative one. It depended on their awareness of a profound union between humanity and divinity and was a logical outgrowth of this perception. It did not create this new sense of intimacy; it was rather its child.

So, too, with the idea of Jesus' Resurrection. Faith in Jesus depends primarily not on the miracle of the Resurrection, but on the sense of the intimacy between humanity and divinity revealed through his ministry and person. He had to rise because he was who he was. His Resurrection was a consequence of what he did while on earth. And what he preached can be summarized as the notion of the Incarnation, his proclamation of the indwelling presence of God in humanity, in a measure that was hinted at in Pharisaic theology but which still did not come out in all its power and glory. So, contrary to Roy Eckardt, I believe that resurrection can be retained in a Christology that wishes to be sensitive to Judaism's continuing salvific role. Without question, the Resurrection doctrine should be cleansed of its triumphalistic dimensions, as Eckardt suggests. Understood as a derivative doctrine of the Incarnation, however, it can remain a powerful statement about the meaning of Jesus as well as about the significance of humanity. Also, understanding that the process begun by the Incarnation remains fundamentally incomplete, resurrection becomes a statement about future promise rather than about present reality. For the notion of resurrection within Pharisaism was intimately tied to the communal ethos of Judaism. No individual in the Pharisaic perspective would rise until the community had reached the end-time. Thus there were no grounds for any triumphalistic outlook along the way. Sin, at its roots the struggle between Creator and creatures for supremacy, would be resolved.

This was the promise of Jesus' Resurrection, but it was not yet fully resolved. And this resolution would happen only if people first cooperated on this earth to resolve the struggles and divisions within humanity.

The actual process of building a Christology in the early Church seemed to have followed along these general lines. After an initial interpretation of Jesus as the one promised by the Jewish Messianic tradition, a viewpoint that dominates the earliest strata of the Gospel materials and the first of the Pauline writings, problems arose within the apostolic Church. These problems had the potential to undermine the faith of the new believing community, for it was becoming apparent that the signs and realities which were to accompany the appearance of the Messiah were nowhere to be seen. Hence the later Paul and especially John were compelled to re-examine the earlier Christologies. Deeper reflection led them to an awareness of new and potentially more important aspects of Jesus as the Christ. As a result of his ministry and the power of his person, the human community acquired a fuller vision of the link that exists, that has always existed, between God and humanity. Divinity and humanity stood in a much more intimate relationship than previous generations had imagined possible. This linkage carried profound implications for the way people needed to relate to one another and to their Father. It also accorded to each individual person a higher sense of dignity. This awareness was definitely tied to the development of the heightened sense of the individual person's dignity which we have seen was one of the hallmarks of the Pharisaic revolution. Nonetheless, in the final analysis we must admit that the Christologies of John and Paul represent a significant advance in this area, compared to the understanding prevalent in Second Temple Judaism.

Incarnational Christology and Pharisaism

No contemporary writer has posited as close a connection between Pharisaic Judaism and Christianity in the "incarnational" area than Ellis Rivkin, though, as we have seen earlier, Clemens Thoma also shows an awareness of the linkage. In Rivkin's view the Pharisaic movement began to question the understanding of history prevalent in Judaism for so long a time. The movement began to shift the focus of salvation from the people and the land to the individual. Integral to this shift was an attempt to strip time and history of their directional thrust:

> History was not moving anywhere. Time present, time forward, time prior, was indistinguishable, in structure and in quality so long as

salvation was attainable. One was no closer to eternal life or resurrection now than had been an Abraham or a Moses then. God was no more the Father now than he had been the Father then. The individual soul had been as precious then as it was now.[172]

Rivkin then goes on to relate this internalization process in Pharisaism to the internalization process involved in the development of later Christology, particularly in its Pauline version. He feels that Paul's notion of Christ is structurally congruent with the Pharisaic system of the salvific Oral/Written Torah:

Each was believed by its devotees to be the creation of God the Father. Each promises to deliver from sin and each offers eternal life and resurrection for the believing individual. Each preaches that Reality is within, not without. Each denies to *externality* the power to refute the certainties of an *internalized* faith. And each acknowledges that the Messiah will come—or come again. But, until that unknown and perhaps unknowable day, salvation is at hand: for the Pharisees in the twofold law; for Paul in the ever-redeeming Christ.[173]

Thus for Rivkin the Pharisaic revolution can be said to have "seeded" the Christian revolution, to have provided it with the emphasis on internalization as it reflected on the meaning of the Christ event. The spiritual power of Christianity is shown, therefore, to be in an important way "an extension of the power of Pharisaism." While Pauline Christology and Pharisaic emphasis on the twofold law may diverge in various respects, they remain "strikingly similar in form, structure, and symbolic power.[174]

This understanding of the internalization process taking place within Judaism in the centuries immediately preceding the birth of Jesus puts the whole effort of internalizing Christology into a somewhat different light. It need not automatically mean a loss by Christians of Judaism's historical sense. Nor can it be presented in a simplistic way as the basis for the separation of Christianity from Judaism. In my view, Rivkin somewhat overdraws the significance of the rethinking of history and the consequent internalization process that took place in Pharisaic Judaism. There is little doubt that this process occurred to some extent, but it did not represent a total rejection of Judaism's more classic sense of history as directional, as Rivkin would want to claim. Rather the Pharisees looked for a new depth in human history while retaining the previous directional thrust. They had come to see the good aspects of the Exodus theology of history as well as its limitations. Somehow individual consciousness and the more personal interior link between God and the individual human person had to be integrated into the theology of history. Thus, while Rivkin is correct in speaking about a fundamental change in the approach to history within Pharisaism, I would disagree with his attempts to portray this change as a complete break with the past outlook of Judaism.

This internalization process with respect to history is something, incidentally, that is missing in the presentations of the Exodus event as liberation, developed by such theologians as Gutierrez and Bonino. While they are to be commended for reintroducing the Exodus concept of history into Christian theology, they need to take greater account of the internalization process in Second Temple Judaism as they link the Exodus event to the liberating power of Christ.

It is also this important link between the internalization process in Judaism and the development of later Christology that Rosemary Ruether overlooks in her theses about the "spiritualizing of the eschatological" and "the historicizing of the eschatological"—processes which in her view account for Christianity's abandonment of its Jewish heritage and eventually for the growth of antisemitism. Ruether is not totally unaware of this process. In *Faith and Fratricide* she writes:

> It is commonplace to speak of Judaism as an historical religion uniquely characterized by the idea of salvation history. But there is a sense in which Pharisaism sought to emancipate the Jew from the tyranny of history, as much as from the tyranny of tribe and national homeland. Just as the spiritual Jew can be a Jew without the land, the temple, or political autonomy to vindicate God's love for him, so he no longer should read history with too much anxiety to be sure that it is going his way, or even that it is very clearly going any place at all. Rabbinic Judaism makes little effort to distinguish history from myth.[175]

However, Ruether never really relates this understanding of internalization to her charge that the spiritualizing and historicizing of the eschatological pushed Christological interpretation in a direction that proved disastrous for the Church's relationship to history and for its attitudes towards the Jewish people. It is a point I raised in an essay dealing with her volume. Her response to the piece continues to circumvent the issue.[176] I think she has made an especially valuable contribution in calling our attention to the potential for disastrous effects that such an internalization of Christology (and by implication of Judaism as well) *can* have and in fact *did* have in the course of Christianity's evolution. But the difference between my position and hers is that she makes the anti-historical and antisemitic attitudes, which neither of us would deny resulted from this internalization process, integral to the process. This would of necessity lead us to the conclusion that these early Christologies are absolutely unredeemable for use in our own time. I would maintain, on the other hand, that those were tragic aberrations from a fundamentally positive development. Thus, while we need to cleanse Christology of these aberrations as quickly as possible (and the process has in fact begun), we can build on the inner-consciousness Christologies of the later Paul and John. Even if Ruether continues to feel that these Christologies are fundamentally inadequate for our day because of a built-in other-worldliness, she must at least admit that the tendency was inherited from an important branch of Judaism. Hence the internalization process, despite the concrete instances of antisemitism for which it was at least partially responsible, cannot be simply described as in total opposition to Judaism, in the way Ruether maintains.

Christology as Manifestation of the Divine-Human Nexus

Returning specifically to the process whereby the Pauline and Johannine internalized Christologies were developed, we face the question: Why the delay in their appearance? In an essay written some time ago, Raymond E. Brown provides some insights into a possible answer. Brown writes:

> If Jesus presented Himself as one in whose life God was active, He did so not primarily by the use of titles, or by clear statements about what He was, but rather by the impact of His person and His life on those who followed Him.[177]

Brown has concluded that the term "God" in reference to Jesus did not appear until the second half of the New Testament period and became frequent only toward the latter part of that epoch. Its origins were probably liturgical. Little or no evidence has been unearthed to date of any reference to Jesus as God within the Jerusalem or Palestinian communities of the first two decades of Christianity. This conclusion, Brown believes, is strengthened by the evidence gathered from the early extra-biblical Christian materials.

In addition to the relative silence about the divine dimensions of Jesus in the earliest strata of the New Testament materials, we can locate passages that explicitly seem to deny the affirmation "Jesus is God." The data at hand seems to show that in the initial stages of the Christian Church the heritage of the Hebrew Scriptures determined the use of the title "God." In this perspective, "God" was a title too narrow to be applied to Jesus, for its point of reference was the Father of Jesus, the God whom Jesus addressed in prayer. Slowly, in the growth of Christian theology, "God" took on a wider significance:

> It was seen that God had revealed so much of Himself in Jesus that "God" had to be able to include both Father and Son. The Pauline works *seem* to fall precisely in this stage of development. . . . By the time of the Pastorals, however, Jesus was well known as God-and-Savior. The Johannine works come from the final years of the century when the usage is common.[178]

It is Brown's contention that the practice of applying the title "God" to Jesus, as was mentioned above, had liturgical origins. This viewpoint is significant for Christological construction, for it means that it took the consciousness-expanding process evoked by liturgy to show the Church the ultimate significance of the Christ event. The New Testament does not use the title "God" in a direct fashion relative to the Jesus of ministry. It was only in-depth reflection on the meaning of the Christ event combined with the experience of God's presence in the liturgy that enabled the early Christian community to understand what Jesus had revealed. And even then they recognized that the crucial revelation was the intimate link between God and humanity that was and that remains. Hence they reserved the term "God" for those times when they were essentially speaking of Christ as the theological expression of this ongoing divine-human nexus, rather than of the person Jesus whose life on earth made this visible to humankind. In the Johannine writings it is only the pre-existent Word or the Son in the Father's presence or the resurrected Jesus who is hailed as God, while the doxologies common to Pauline writings acknowledge as God only the triumphant Jesus. In the Letter to the Hebrews, the stress is on the Jesus whose throne is forever.

With the research of Brown serving as a confirmation of the notion of a developmental Christology in the early Church in which the Incarnational dimension was a product of the later stages, we can now turn our attention to a positive articulation of Christology in light of this developmental theory. Put somewhat simply, what ultimately came to be recognized with clarity for the first time through the ministry and person of Jesus was how profoundly integral humanity was to the self-definition of

God. This in turn implied that each human person is somehow divine, that he or she somehow shares in the constitutive nature of God. Christ is the theological symbol that the Church selected to try to express this reality. As we have discovered from a study of the later strata of the New Testament materials, this humanity existed in the Godhead from the very beginning. Thus in a very real sense one can say that God did not become man in Jesus. God always was man; humanity was an integral part of the Godhead from the beginning. The Christ event was crucial, however, for the manifestation of this reality to the world.

The above statement, it should be made clear, does not mean to simply equate God with the totality of humanity. A gulf remains between God and the human community that is forever impassable. Moreover, in spite of the intimate link with God made known to us through the Christ event, humankind remains equally conscious of the fact that this God is the ultimate Creator of that human life he decided to share with men and women as a gift. Nor does it mean that there was not a uniqueness about the manner in which humanity and divinity were united in Jesus. Human-kind could never have come to the full awareness of the ultimate link between itself and God without the express revelation occasioned by the Christ event. While this event will allow us to experience a new closeness with the Creator God, our humanity will never share the same intimacy with the divine nature that existed in the person of Jesus.

The Christ event was in a sense the culmination of another process. In the act of creation a part of the humanity in the Godhead broke out into a separate, though not fully separated, existence. The new humanity imme-diately had to face the question of its self-identity, especially insofar as that identity related to the Creator God. This is the ultimate struggle taking place in the Book of Genesis. In the period from creation to the Christ event the human community was searching for an authentic self-under-standing that would recognize both the individuality and the divinity of every person. Frequently this led to attempts to assume a stance of superiority over the Father, to a belief in self-divinization in an ultimate sense. Liberation had become self-tyranny. The Christ event once and for all put this process on the right track. It revealed the incomparable greatness of the human person as well as his or her limits. It made these limits tolerable, if not meaningful, because in the suffering of the Son of God it likewise revealed the vulnerability of God. We will have more to say in this regard in the next chapter.

In the Incarnation that growing sense of human uniqueness and dignity, initially expressed in the Genesis theology of the human person as

God's co-creator and further developed in the Pharisaic emphasis on the worth and status of each individual person, reached its zenith. The human person now realized that he or she shared in the very life and existence of God. The human person was still creature; there remained that gulf between humanity in people and humanity in the Godhead. But it was clear that a direct link also existed; the two humanities could touch. The human struggle for self-identity vis-à-vis the Creator God had come to an end in principle, though its full realization still lay ahead. In this sense we can truly say that Christ brought and continues to bring humankind salvation in its root meaning—wholeness. With a proper understanding of the meaning of the Christ event men and women can be healed; they can finally overcome the primal sin of pride—the desire to supplant the Creator in power and status—because they have seen in the Cross the self-imposed limitations of the Father. People now see that their destiny is to live forever in their uniqueness and individuality. God will not finally try to absorb them totally back into his being. In fact it has become apparent that God must allow men and women this degree of eternal distinctiveness in order to reach full maturity himself, to become finally and fully God.

Dialogical Implications of Incarnational Christology

Several additional observations are necessary to put this articulation of Incarnational Christology into a fully proper perspective. While I want to maintain the distinction between Pharisaic Judaism's perception of the link between humanity and divinity, I also want to reaffirm their relationship. As Ellis Rivkin has staunchly maintained, the core of the Pharisaic revolution consists in a firm and unwavering belief in what he terms "an alluring Triad":

> (1) God the Just and Caring Father so loved each and every individual that (2) He revealed to Israel His twofold law—written and oral—which, when *internalized* and faithfully obeyed, (3) promises to the Law-abiding individual eternal life for his soul and resurrection for his body. Internalization of the divine will as the ultimate, the most certain, and the only enduring reality—this was the grand achievement of the Scribes-Pharisees.[179]

This Triad seeded the Christian revolution and provided the roots for the vision of an internalized religion. To repeat a statement made earlier in this chapter, the power of Christianity can thus be described as in a real way an extension of the power inherent in the Pharisaic revolution. This is particularly true for Pauline thought:

> Paul's certainty that Christ was resurrected was rooted in the certainty that there could be a resurrection. Paul's Father is the Father of the Scribes-Pharisees. . . . Paul's internalized Christ is the counterpart of the internalized twofold Law of the Pharisees; Paul's hope for eternal life and resurrection is the Pharisaic hope. Paul's unwavering faith in Scripture is one and the same as the faith of the Scribes-Pharisees.[180]

So runs the comparative thinking of Rivkin. There are two major drawbacks in his approach. The first is an overstress on the Pharisaic abandonment of external history as a source of religious meaning and value. The Pharisees were trying to add depth to the concept of history with their internalization process, not engaging in a wholesale abandonment of a powerful tradition in pre-Pharisaic Judaism, as Rivkin seems to imply.

Second, Rivkin does not sufficiently stress the gulf between Christianity and Judaism relative to the Incarnation. Without doubt his scholarly contributions have helped to break down the stereotypical view that the development of Incarnational Christology has absolutely no connection with the Judaism of its time. It is in the writings of Abraham Joshua Heschel that we find at least a partial affirmation of the same thrust as in Rivkin regarding Incarnation, yet also an unequivocal statement about the fundamental differences that remain. For Heschel there is little doubt that the notion of the Incarnation is the point at which Christianity and Judaism part company spiritually, despite the presence in Judaism of a certain measure of "Incarnationalism." The biblical scholar James A. Sanders has spoken of this dimension of Heschel's thought.[181] But Heschel himself quite strongly maintains that his notion of the "sympathetic union" which is central to his interpretation of the prophets is to be clearly distinguished on the one hand from the mystical union where the person attains a state of identity with the divine and, on the other, from the notion of the Incarnation where the divine becomes human.[182] The human personality is not annihilated by the divine essence. At this point Heschel and Incarnational Christology stand in complete agreement. But neither can the human personality in any way be identified with the divine essence. Here is where the fundamental disagreement between Christianity and Judaism comes to the fore. All that is possible from the Jewish perspective as interpreted by Heschel is a profound feeling of solidarity with the divine purpose—one that results in a new type of divine-human partnership in which attainment of God's aims becomes inextricably linked to human cooperation and effort. Incarnational Christology does affirm this as well, but it affirms something more.

The second observation following from the Incarnational Christology sketched above has to do with the basic dignity accorded to each individual person. This dignity can never be erased no matter what sin the person may have committed. This point was stressed over and over again by Jesus in his public ministry. Obviously this understanding will have many practical consequences in the realm of ethics. Following from this understanding is a concomitant realization that since the basis for individual dignity is to be located in the presence within the person of God's very life, no person can perpetually reject another, cannot cast him or her out of his or her presence forever. In other words, Incarnational Christology insofar as it has implications for anthropology is inherently communal. This is why Jesus continually underlined the centrality of reconciliation during his public ministry and preached the love of enemies which, as we noted above, the Jewish scholar David Flusser acknowledged as one of the most distinctive features of Jesus' teaching. Because we are indeed far from a realization of such communion we must say that the Christ event is far from its full activation.

The Social Dimensions of Incarnational Christology

The realization of this incompleteness forces believing Christians into a certain framework which insures that an authentic Incarnational theology will not fall into the trap of false mysticism and exaggerated individualism. Rosemary Ruether has made this criticism of me in a recent commentary on my Christological approach. She writes:

> Pawlikowski would mystify the question by leaping to the other pole of the Christian denial of the messianic question: namely to spiritualization of salvation. This is the way of privatistic mystical or pietist Christianity which solves the problem of unredeemed history by ignoring it. Since our souls are saved, who cares what happens to our bodies, to the body politic, to the cosmic body?[183]

Other colleagues such as Professor Franklin Littell and J. Coert Rylaarsdam have raised similar questions, though in a somewhat more approving tone. Both express some concern that I might be in danger of losing that Jewish sense of rootedness in history which each considers to be integral to any responsible notion of human salvation. Rylaarsdam, for example, has suggested that the "Word made flesh" might prove a better term than "Incarnational Christology" since it better captures the activist sense of the Incarnation.

I welcome these critiques because I wish to safeguard at all costs any false interpretation of my approach. Too often Incarnational Christology has led to anti-social attitudes on the part of Christians. This is far from what I have in mind. The Incarnational Christology that I advocate must ultimately be understood as the revelation to the human family that its humanity can be made whole because of the ability of people to be touched in the deepest realms of their consciousness by the humanity of God and its saving power. This gives history a vital new significance. For what men and women are doing in and through the historical process is trying to establish political and social structures that will enhance the consciousness of people and bring about the possibility of their ultimate communion while preserving some degree of individuality and uniqueness. Social and political structures are a reflection of human consciousness; they also aid or detract from the growth of human consciousness. This is the insight captured by Teilhard de Chardin when he wrote:

> Note this well: I attribute no definite and absolute value to the various constructions of man. I believe that they will disappear, recast in a new whole that we cannot yet conceive. At the same time I admit that they have an essential provisional role—that they are necessary, inevitable phases through which we (we or the race) must pass in the course of our metamorphosis. What I love in them is not their particular form, but their function which is to build up, in some mysterious way, first something divinizable—and then, through the grace of Christ alighting on our effort, something divine.[184]

There are two key points to be grasped. First, there exists an intimate link between history and human consciousness. This is the deepening sense of history that began with the Pharisaic movement in Judaism and which both the liberation theologians and Rosemary Ruether fail to deal with in an adequate fashion. Second, salvation in the final analysis involves the ability to establish communion with God and neighbor through the healing which results from greater contact between human consciousness and the humanity of God as a consequence of the destruction of dehumanizing socio-political structures. Socio-political structures which establish patterns of oppression and injustice thus block the realization of that depth of human consciousness where salvation and the final Kingdom are ultimately to be located.

This understanding of Christology, which stresses the power inherent in the link between human consciousness and the humanity of God that the Pharisaic revolution and Incarnational Christology brought to the surface, also provides the realistic grounds for faith in the ability to achieve the communion and wholeness of the final Kingdom. Edward Schillebeeckx captures this insight well in the following words:

> The heart of the message of Christ's death and resurrection unto eternity lies in the proclamation that, by virtue of the Christ event, it is indeed possible to build up humanity and that this is not a labor of Sisyphus. In biblical terms this possibility is maintained over against all human despair, when we say that this is the grace of God's kingdom being achieved in man's world; it is the kingdom of justice, peace, and love, a kingdom where there will be no evil, nor mourning, nor crying, nor pain.[185]

Connections with Other Systematic Christologies

The Christological approach offered above has many close connections with that presented by John Paul II in his first encyclical *Redemptor Hominis*.[186] In an excellent analysis of this document Gregory Baum emphasizes the uniqueness and importance of its Christological vision. As Baum interprets it, the Pope insists:

> Because of God's act in Jesus Christ the Church must respect the dignity of persons, defend their rights as human beings, and summon people to involve themselves in political action so that these rights will be respected. In other words, the Church's concern with human rights is not part of a humanitarian mission, based on natural law, related to its essential supernatural mission in a subordinate manner. The Church's solicitude for human well-being is in fact an exercise of its supernatural mission, founded upon its Christological doctrine.[187]

John Paul II appears to see in the notion of divine grace an historical dimension. This grace is not merely the source of personal unity between creature and Creator but an enabling force that renders men and women responsible historical agents for the transformation of life on this earth. Put another way, says Baum, in *Redemptor Hominis* "the spiritual is historical. The divine summons empowering people to enter into holiness does not thereby lift them out of their historical situation and make them ready for an invisible world, but leaves them in their historical place and appoints them to be agents of Christ in their troubled societies."[188]

Where the Christological vision laid out in this chapter would differ somewhat with that of the encyclical is in placing a greater emphasis on the communal basis of human existence (the Pope overfocuses on the individual person) and in stressing the connection between Incarnational Christology and Second Temple Judaism. This latter is something that John Paul II totally overlooks.

As for some of the other Christologies examined previously in this volume, the following comments are in order. The Christologies of Schillebeeckx and Fiorenza show the best possibilities for development within the Christian-Jewish dialogue. Both need a great deal of correction and addition relative to the understanding of the Jewish roots of Christianity. Both could likewise profit from the emphasis on the salvific dimensions of the Exodus experience that liberationists like Gutierrez bring out. Schillebeeckx needs to give much greater attention to the social justice dimensions of Christology as well. E. P. Sanders, while on to something important in his contrast between Judaism and Christianity as different styles of religion, overplays this distinction. Participation in the redeeming presence of God is at the heart of Torah for the Pharisaic-rabbinic approach to religion as Abraham Heschel and Ellis Rivkin have shown. Sanders does not do sufficient justice to this fact. But despite these criticisms it is these three theologians who have in a special way provided important theological substance for the dialogue. The Christologies of such people as Pannenberg, Moltmann, Küng, Sobrino and Boff remain unusable, on the other hand, without fundamental changes despite the deep sensitivity of some like Moltmann and Küng to the tragic dimensions of the historic Christian-Jewish relationship.

Incarnational Christology and Jewish Continuity

The above exposition of the meaning of Christology leads inevitably to the question: What significance does the Jewish covenant retain? This is not an easy question since the Christological vision presented in this chapter does imply a degree of universalism. Yet, while all problems have not been solved, it is necessary to assert that Judaism continues to play a unique and distinctive role in the process of human salvation. Despite the biblical heritage that they share and other similarities, Judaism and Christianity are essentially distinct religions, each emphasizing different but complementary aspects of human religiosity. This would support the contention of such Jewish scholars as Arthur Cohen and Hans Jonas that reference to a single Judaeo-Christian tradition represents a basic distortion of reality. Whatever might have been ideally, the fact is that Judaism and Christianity went their separate ways. In the course of history they have each developed a unique ethos. Authentic dialogue between them must start with the clear recognition of this difference. I think this is the point that E. P. Sanders was basically trying to bring out in his suggested contrast despite the limitations of his approach.

Among the unique features of Judaism is its sense of peoplehood, of community, the belief that no individual person can achieve salvation until the whole human family has attained salvation. Part of this is rooted in the sense of peoplehood that is integral to the Exodus covenant. That is why it is so significant that Gutierrez and Bonino have brought back this notion as authentic revelation for their Christology, even though their handling of the event needs significant improvement. And that improvement must move along the lines advanced by A. Roy Eckardt who has stated forcefully and correctly in his volume *Elder and Younger Brothers:*

> If there is a true sense in which God has manifested himself uniquely in Jesus of Nazareth, it must be said that the mystery of this divine act is in principle no greater than the sacred acts through which Israel was originally elected.[189]

The revelation at Sinai stands on equal footing with the revelation in Jesus. Unfortunately Christianity frequently lost sight of this revelatory sense of community given at Sinai since it separated itself from the Synagogue. Perhaps under the influence of Hellenistic thought where concern for the individual predominated, the Church's interpretation of the Christ event became more and more individualistic in the bad sense of the term. It turned increasingly to an I-God relationship in which people believed they could reach full communion with God without achieving communion with the rest of humanity.

One prime example of this tendency was the practice of the Eucharist that has only been reversed since Vatican Council II. The Eucharist stands as the ultimate symbol in the Church that people can only be saved communally. It is a recognition that people united become in a very real way the body of Christ. This is an integral part of the mature Paul's Christology. It represents one of his most important statements about the unity of the human family, the dignity of humanity and the ultimate link between humanity and divinity. Yet this symbol, unlike the sabbath meal in which it had its origins, was allowed to deteriorate into a privatistic I-God action. Here is a clear, concrete example of a difference in ethos between Judaism and Christianity. Christian contact with Judaism is necessary for Christians to overcome this deep-seated and long-standing tendency toward false privatization of religion.

Second, the Church's Christological tradition lost sight of the sense of the human person as co-creator, as responsible for history and for the world God created. Part of this irresponsibility was due to a continuation of the older Christology which claimed that Christ had brought about the Messianic Kingdom. But it was likewise due to the fact that most Christians had lost sight of the notion that salvation is ultimately communal, that one cannot by-pass other people in trying to achieve unity with God. There was little understanding that God resided within the human family. Here is another area where contact with Judaism will prove of immense benefit to Christian theology.

Third, there is the vision of God as a person active in history. This characteristic of Hebrew theodicy may seem rather commonplace until we recognize how strongly some of the liberation theologians insist upon it as pivotal to a recovery of a social justice outlook in theology. Too often Christians have abandoned their Hebraic heritage in this regard in favor of a Greek philosophical image of God as the unmoved Mover, as changeless Being. In so doing the Church has tended to identify authentic piety with solitude and quiet, for these after all seemed to be most strongly characteristic of the Godhead. In this atmosphere action to root out injustice tended to become secondary in Christology with at best a minor relationship to authentic Christian piety. There is a significant, even profound, difference between historical Christianity and historical Judaism on this score. We should be grateful to theologians like Gutierrez for bringing the Hebraic notion of God back into Christian spirituality. Without it there is every chance that the Incarnational Christology we have described in this chapter will fall into that false Christological mysticism that Rosemary Ruether has so strongly and correctly condemned.

But despite the very important contributions made by Gutierrez and Bonino in bringing back the Exodus covenant and the activist image of God into Christian theology, they show a dark side as well. It is their failure to fully appreciate the role of Torah in liberation. The criticism of Leon Klenicki in this regard, cited earlier, needs to be repeated here. Too often the Christian liberation in Jesus is too general. Liberation cannot become fully implemented in a society until it has been transformed into socio-cultural structures. This is what the process of Torah was all about. Jesus himself, as a son of the Pharisaic revolution, was certainly aware of the need for this. But later Christian thought too often forgot this fact, thereby abandoning the quest for justice, the struggle against social structural sin, that is central to any authentic Christology. The Christian-Jewish dialogue by enabling Christians to truly understand the function of Torah can help the Church move away from mere generalized statements about the freedom found in Christ Jesus to action that creates liberating structures in our society. How often do Christians naively express a preference for the unspecified statements about freedom in Christ over the minute details found in the Hebrew Scriptures, not realizing that without such concretizations the Christian sense of freedom in Christ will prove terribly ineffective.

The final characteristic of Judaism that needs to be highlighted in a contrast with Christianity is its sense of the goodness of creation. One could never assert that this dimension has been totally lacking in Christianity. There is, for example, the creational theology of the Franciscan tradition which had considerable impact in the history of theology and piety. Yet, overall, Judaism has retained a much more consistent and firm commitment to the notion that God's image shines through his creation. Too many influential theological trends in Christian history played down the goodness of creation. Thus while it would certainly be falsifying history to project any absolute difference between Judaism and Christianity in this area, nonetheless the Jewish ethos can serve as a powerful stimulus for the reawakening of creational theology in substantial segments of the Christian community where it has been largely dormant.

Looking at the contrast between Judaism and Christianity from the latter's perspective, the notion of Incarnational Christology developed in this chapter has pushed the Church's ethos in a somewhat different direction than Judaism. First of all, the stress on the individual person has been far greater. Here James Parkes is definitely on target in his contrast. This is not to say that Judaism lacks concern for the individual. We are speaking rather of the degree of emphasis. Much of modern Judaism has inherited the general Western concern for individual rights, but I am not sure that this has been clearly related to traditional Jewish theology. There is, for example, nothing quite equivalent in Judaism to Vatican II's *Declaration on Religious Liberty* or John Paul II's *Redemptor Hominis* where the individual person in his or her absolute dignity becomes the very basis for theological construction and ethical reflection. I am not one to claim that Christianity has always been faithful to this stress on the individual's dignity, either externally or in its internal operations. But I think there are different theological starting points on the question of the individual person's role and rights in Judaism and Christianity that could be explored further for mutual profit in the dialogue. Now that Jews have political sovereignty in Israel and have to deal with issues of minority rights, Christian theology may have a contribution to make to Jewish self-understanding in this regard.

Incarnational Christology and the Particularity-Universality Tension

Another area where Christianity's Incarnational Christology makes some difference is in resolving the universality-particularity tension common to most religious traditions. At the outset I wish to clearly repudiate the traditional way of stating the contrast within Christianity: Judaism is particularistic in orientation and hence inferior; Christianity is universalistic and hence superior. This is simply a gross oversimplification of what Judaism stands for in theory and how Christianity has acted in practice.

The universalistic/particularistic question has been struggled with by Jewish religious teachers from biblical times to the present day.[190] Therefore it is completely erroneous for Christians to assume, as they have for so long a time, that Judaism represents particularity pure and simple.

Professor Jacob Neusner has strongly challenged the validity of the Christian stereotypical view of Judaism with respect to the particularity issue. He claims that upon examining Christian theologies on Judaism in late antiquity, we derive an amusing irony. Proof is abundant that Christians eagerly set out to show themselves as an ethnic group, a new people formed out of the people of this world into the congregation of the Lord, replacing the old congregation of Israel. In actual fact Christians East and West admired the highly ethnic character and loyalty of Jewry. The claim on the part of the Church to constitute the "new Israel" was, in Nuesner's words,

> . . . not merely an effort to find a share in the Hebrew Scriptures or to take over the prophecies and promises of the Jews' holy books. It was rather a very serious effort, central to Christian theology on the Church itself, to demonstrate that through Christ Christians came to constitute an ethnic group, Israel, no different from the ethnic group formerly formed by Jewry.[191]

Putting ancient history aside, it would seem that even in the modern period the term "Jew" has produced better social integration of people from diverse ethnic and racial backgrounds than the term "Christian." The term "Jew" has become a primary source of identification that has generally transcended racial and ethnic backgrounds. "Christian" in the meantime has generally served only as a secondary source of identification which has given way to racial, ethnic and nationalistic identities, especially in times of social stress. The tremendous population imbalance existing between Jews and Christians worldwide tends to automatically reinforce the particularity-universality thesis. Hence it is important for Christian thinkers to break through initial impressions on this question.

Theologically I believe that there is some validity in contrasting Judaism and Christianity through the universal-particular model, Jacob Neusner notwithstanding. The Pauline "In Christ there is neither Jew nor Greek" contains an important religious nuance. But we need to explore it much more thoroughly than we have thus far. By starting with the solemn commitment to peoplehood, Judaism has to struggle with the problem of the outsider; by beginning with the individual, Christianity has to struggle with how it can also maximize its communitarian ideal. The starting points are different for each faith community, but the questions that each must face are not all that dissimilar.

Initial analysis would seem to warrant the contention that Christianity has better maintained the "universal" as ideal, but that in reality Judaism has done a somewhat better job in overcoming tribalism than Christianity. We have discovered so often, most dramatically in the Holocaust and in the racial conflict in the United States, how deeply tribalism still holds sway over the minds and hearts of supposedly "universalistic" Christians. It may be that in light of Incarnational Christology the Church needs to build its sense of universalism upon the dignity of each individual man and woman. This is what John Paul II's theology seems to be saying. Yet, as the liberation theologians have been constantly insisting, Christianity's communal mandate also needs to be realized. In addition there is the increasing recognition since Vatican II's *Constitution on the Church in the Modern World* that cultural diversity has to be a part of Christian self-expression. There is also the fact that with the growth of secularism and non-Christian philosophies and religions Christianity may soon come to approximate Judaism's minority standing. The world scene is no longer dominated by Christian nations as it once was. Christianity's long cherished dream of converting the whole world, of bringing all the peoples of the earth into the Church's fold, has been shattered. Christians have not really assimilated this into their consciousness as yet; when they do, it may prove to have a significant impact on the notion of Christian universalism.

It will become clear that the Church's understanding of universal people-hood will need significant revision. That is why a statement such as that of Professor Tomaso Federici which rejects undue proselytism of Jews in favor of dialogue (we will discuss this question further in Chapter 7) has implications far beyond the Christian-Jewish dialogue.[192] The old goal of achieving universalism through the baptism of all races and nations is no longer a possibility. The only realistic path to universality now is through dialogue with peoples of other faiths and ideologies.

In the coming decades Christianity will have to face the problem of public value maintenance and of group identity in societies in which the old cultural/societal props for the Church's teachings are collapsing, and also to find a way of preserving a sense of unity among its diverse ethnic and racial memberships. In both these areas the experience of Judaism can prove of help to Christianity. And both Christianity and Judaism will have to learn to relate to the Asian and African religions, to Islam and to the various forms of Marxism. In this endeavor Christianity has taken the lead and Judaism could learn from its successes and failures thus far.

Incarnational Christology and the Jewish Land Tradition

A final area of difference between Christianity and Judaism resulting from the Church's acceptance of Incarnational Christology concerns the question of land. The land tradition has been an integral part of Jewish religious self-identity since biblical times. Psalm 147, for example, speaks of the Lord rebuilding Jerusalem where the dispersed of Israel will gather, where the brokenhearted will be healed and the wounds of the suffering will be looked after. The late theologian Rabbi Abraham Heschel, one of the giants of twentieth century Jewish thought, has captured this tradition-al feeling in Judaism in his volume *Israel: An Echo of Eternity.* As Heschel explains it, Israel, and especially its heart—the city of Jerusalem—holds an almost mystical meaning for Jews:

> Jerusalem is more than a place in space . . . a memorial to the past. Jerusalem is a prelude, an anticipation of days to come. . . . It is not our memory, our past that ties us to the land. It is our future. Spiritually, I am a native of Jerusalem. I have prayed here all my life. My hopes have their home in these hills. . . . Jerusalem is never at the end of the road. She is the city where waiting for God was born.[193]

The hopeful longing for a return to the land of Israel sustained the spirit of the Jewish people during their nineteen centuries of enforced, often bitter, exile. This dream of going back was recalled each year at the conclusion of the Passover Seder meal. The prayer of the people spoke their deep feelings, "Next year in Jerusalem."

After this Jewish hope for a return to Zion became thinkable once again in actual political terms toward the close of the last century, Jewish writers in great numbers set out to reinterpret this hope in a modern setting. Some eventually concluded that diaspora existence, life outside the land of Israel, should be looked upon as the ideal goal for contemporary Jews. In effect, they urged the burial of the traditional longing for the land of Israel as a modern dream. Many members of the Reform movement in Judaism endorsed this position during the early years of discussion regarding the re-establishment of a Jewish state. Surveying the various works dealing with Zionism, Manfred Vogel has delineated five principal trends in Jewish thought regarding Judaism's relationship to the land.[194] The first is the philosophical-religious thrust that basically articulated the land covenant in theological or philosophical categories rather than in political or ideological terms.

The second is the Zionist ideological trend that clearly expressed the link between peoplehood and land in cultural and political categories. Next we find the cultural autonomist position which championed diaspora existence over settlement in the land of Israel. The fourth approach was dominated by socialist categories. The return to the land was seen in the context of advancing the general world goals of the socialist movement. Some socialist Jews embraced Zionism as a result. They had as their goal a socialist political order in any new Jewish state that might emerge. Other socialist-minded Jews were convinced that socialism demanded that Jews affirm diaspora existence in multi-cultural societies. Finally, there was the mystical trend. It tried to articulate the relationship between peoplehood and land in mystical categories.

It is not possible here to explore each of these trends in their particularities. Overall, Vogel's research has led him to conclude that the majority of Jewish attempts at self-identity affirm the category of land as central. And, as a result of shattering events like the Nazi Holocaust and the recent Arab-Israeli wars, this affirmation has grown in recent years to the point of virtual unanimity.

There is one aspect of Vogel's analysis that needs special attention. It is his contention that the fundamental category for most of the Jewish writers dealing with Zionism was peoplehood, not land. Essential to the notion of Jewish peoplehood was the sense of working toward redemption, of seeing the consummation of that redemption, in the dimension of time. The category of land entered the structure of Jewish faith in a secondary and derivative way: it was implied in the meaning of peoplehood. In order to fulfill its redemptive vocation, the Jewish people require sovereignty— the power to regulate their life in both its internal and its external phases. Without sovereignty and the freedom to decide and direct the life of community, the category of peoplehood would become an empty ideal. The Jewish people would realistically be unable to carry out the redemptive task assigned to them.

But sovereignty can be attained only by a people in possession of a land. Thus it should be clear that while the category of land is secondary and derivative in terms of Judaism's basic faith outlook, land is in fact no less essential than peoplehood with respect to the carrying out of Israel's redemptive vocation. Without a land in which sovereignty can be exercised, the fulfillment (and even the very workings) of the redemptive vocation is simply unthinkable for Jews. It is true that Jewish faith can, and has in fact, survived the absence of land, something that would prove impossible if the category of peoplehood were lost. But this survival amounted to a truncated form of existence. In Vogel's words, "In dia-spora-existence Judaism could only mark time. It could only, so to speak, hold the fort. For the resumption of the active pursuit of its redemptive vocation it had to await and hope for the restoration of the land."[195]

With the actual re-establishment of the State of Israel in 1948, the centuries-long yearning of the Jewish community became reality. As in any polyglot community, not all contemporary Jews, including those residing in Israel itself, understand the significance of the state in the same way. Some view it in explicitly religious categories, as the start of the eschatological in-gathering of the exiles. Others look upon its establishment as an affirmation of life and hope after the death and destruction wrought upon the Jewish people by the Nazi Holocaust. They sometimes speak of it as the ultimate Jewish victory over Hitler. Emil Fackenheim has said that after the experience of the Holocaust the survival of Israel assumes the status of the 614th commandment of the Torah. It is the only avenue open to Jews today to insure that Hitler will not achieve a posthumous victory. The majority of Jews in Israel, victims of persecution in Hitler's Germany, in Arab countries, and in the Soviet Union have experienced it as a place of survival where they can enjoy a new life in dignity and freedom. But even those Israelis who choose not to interpret Israel in strictly religious terms tend, in their so-called secular language and terminology, to echo the spirit of the land tradition that permeates the Hebrew Scriptures and the rabbinic tradition.

As Christians approach the study of the land tradition in Judaism and its expression in contemporary Israel, several questions come to the fore. Is this religious concern about the land of Israel a part of the historic Jewish commitment to salvation within history? This seems to be one implication of Vogel's analysis. Is the general inability of Christians to understand the Jewish perception of the land of Israel the result of an abandonment of a sense of history by Christian theology? Has a vision of a "heavenly Jerusalem" so emasculated Christian awareness of God's salvific action within history that it is impossible for the Church today to identify in a meaningful way with the spirit of the Hebrew Scriptures? What function, if any, does Israel play in Christian Christological understanding in our time?

In dealing with these questions Christians need to begin with the pioneering work of such Christian biblical scholars as W. D. Davies, John Townsend and Walter Brueggemann. While there are differences in their perspectives, they nonetheless seem to agree (1) that the New Testament does not clearly eliminate Judaism's historic claim to the land, and (2) that land remains important for Christian self-expression, at least to the extent that the process of salvation in Christianity is deeply imbedded in the flow of human history.

Brueggemann is perhaps the strongest of these voices regarding the continued significance of the biblical land tradition for *both* Jews and Christians today. The interpretation of Scripture has thrived, he asserts, on the false construction of antitheses between space/time and nature/history. Time and history were generally looked upon as distinctive Hebrew categories. He rejects such projections. In the Hebrew Scriptures we find no timeless space nor spaceless time. There is rather what he terms "storied place," a locale which takes its meaning from the history it has witnessed:

> There are stories which have authority because they are located in a place. This means that biblical faith cannot be presented simply as an historical movement indifferent to place which could have happened in one setting as well as another, because it is undeniably fixed in this place with this meaning. And for all its apparent "spiritualizing," the New Testament does not escape this rootage. The Christian tradition has been very clear in locating the story in Bethlehem, Nazareth, Jerusalem, and Galilee.[196]

Brueggemann insists that the antithesis of the God of history over against the gods of the land is outdated. Yahweh is pictured as Lord of historical events as well as fructifier of the land. He is a fertility God who gives life as well as an historical God who saves and judges. He remains Lord of places as well as of times. Such an understanding casts serious doubts about the validity of the existentialist approach to biblical interpretation identified with scholars such as Rudolf Bultmann. This school of thought has exercised a strong and unfortunate influence in modern biblical interpretation. It wrongly tried to liberate the New Testament from the biblical land tradition in favor of personal meaning for the individual believer acquired through instantaneous and radical decisions of obedience. It is obvious that such Christian interpretation differs sharply with current Jewish reflection on the significance of the State of Israel. Brueggemann is convinced that such an approach must be finally discarded because it has been judged unsound by contemporary research. It represents a fundamental misunderstanding of biblical categories.

The central problem for Brueggemann "is not emancipation but *rootage,* not meaning but *belonging,* not separation from community but *location* within it, not isolation from others but *placement* deliberately between the generation of promise and fulfillment."[197] Both the Hebrew Scriptures and the New Testament present homelessness as the central human problem. They seek to respond to it in terms of promise and gift. Thus a truly faithful Christian will have to incorporate land as a principal category in his or her belief system every bit as much as a believing Jew.

W. D. Davies, in his massive study of the land tradition entitled *The Gospel and the Land,* is stronger than Brueggemann in insisting on a difference between Judaism and Christianity in this respect. Davies insists that with regard to the land promises in the Hebrew Bible the New Testament must be classified as ambivalent. There exist strata within the New Testament materials that look upon the land tradition in a critical light. One actually rejects it outright (Acts 7). But there are other passages in which the land, the Temple and Jerusalem, in an actual geographic, not spiritual sense, are viewed positively. In these passages the land tradition definitely retains a significance for the proclamation of the Christian Gospel.

As Davies sees it, the New Testament presents a twofold witness. On one hand, it transcends the land, Jerusalem, the Temple. Yet its history and theology cannot escape all concern about these realities. In the New Testament, says Davies, holy space is to be found wherever Christ is or has been:

> It personalizes "holy space" in Christ, who, as a figure of history, is rooted in the land; he cleansed the Temple and died in Jerusalem, and

lends his glory to these and to the places where he was, but, as living
Lord, he is also free to move wherever he wills. To do justice to the
personalism of the New Testament, that is, to its Christocentricity, is to
find the clue to the various strata of tradition that we have traced and to
the attitudes they reveal: to their freedom from space and their attach-
ment to spaces.[198]

John Townsend limits his investigation to the question whether the
New Testament rules out the continuation of the Jewish land promises as a
matter of Christian belief. Though he admits that the question is a difficult
one and not directly addressed by the New Testament writers, indirect
references in certain parts of the New Testament do reveal attitudes which
suggest a certain acceptance of the land promises as a continuing valid
heritage belonging to Israel "according to the flesh." Jesus certainly acted,
according to Townsend, in ways that would naturally have led his contemporaries to understand him as one who would help in fulfilling the land
promises central to the Jewish covenant by restoring the land fully to
Israel. There is little reason in his mind to doubt that Jesus was at least in
partial sympathy with such an interpretation of his message even though
he never began any armed rebellion as did other nationalists. But this is as
far as Townsend is willing to go on the question. Unlike Brueggemann and
Davies he is unwilling to offer any possible meaning of the land promises
for Christian faith. The one option not open to Christians, however, is to
claim, as many have, that the New Testament has wiped out Jewish claims
to the land after the Christ event.[199]

    In summary judgment about these three positions, we can say that
they are all correct in ruling out any simple disposal of the Jewish land
tradition by the Gospel message. The rootedness in history that both
Brueggemann and Davies see as a primary legacy of the land tradition and
a continuing need for the Church today is a most welcome development.
Brueggemann, however, does not seem to make enough of a distinction
between Jewish and Christian understandings of the land tradition. Davies
appears nearer the truth in this regard even though his formulation of the
difference may require further nuancing and qualification. While Christianity would sacrifice an essential component of its own self-identity by
eliminating the land tradition from its belief system, it would also stand to
lose some of its distinctiveness were it to appropriate this Jewish tradition
wholly in the way suggested by Brueggemann. Reflection on the difference
between Judaism and Christianity vis-à-vis the land tradition remains an
ongoing need within the Christian scholarly community. It is not a

question of Christianity being anti-land as a result of its acceptance of Incarnational Christology. Loss of the land tradition leads Christianity into a false mysticism that leaves it a skeleton of its true self. But Christianity in principle accords no higher value to one piece of land over another. There is no such reality as a diaspora Christianity. The land of Israel, despite its ties to the life of Jesus, cannot theologically, in light of the sense of universalism inherent in Incarnational Christology, play the same role in Christianity as it does in Judaism.

Here I would personally part company with some colleagues in the dialogue. It is not to say that Judaism's dedication to the land of Israel is perverted. It is only to assert that Christianity and Judaism share a different vision in this regard. It is my contention that Incarnational Christology with its focus on the individual person's dignity does imply a certain rejection of the land tradition as developed in Jewish religious teaching. This theological difference, however, in no way implies that Christians are called to be anti-Israel. On the contrary, there exist compelling reasons for Christianity's support of the State of Israel on moral grounds.

Is Christ the Savior?

One additional point needs to be addressed here. It is that raised by Michael McGarry in his commentary on my previous writings on Christology. He contends that in concert with Rosemary Ruether I emphasize the role of Christ as revealer "without describing how Christ might be Savior or in what way Christians can understand the Resurrection."[200] The second part of his question to me has been dealt with previously in this volume. The "Savior" dimension of the Christological outlook developed in this chapter does need some further elaboration.

I would begin with the premise that the term "salvation" in its root meaning means wholeness. In this sense it is quite legitimate to assert that the understanding and experience of the Christ event brings to the human community the promise and partial fulfillment of salvation. The human community can achieve wholeness or salvation only insofar as it attains total reconciliation both with God and with humankind. This process of reconciliation began at the level of community with the revelation of God in the Sinai covenant. It was developed at the individual level starting with the Pharisaic revolution and achieved a significant new phase in the Christ event. The ultimate contest between humanity and divinity had been settled in a harmonious fashion, at least in principle. Pride had been fully vanquished. The human community could now more easily accept its dependence on God as a gift, for God had acknowledged the dignity of humanity through his presence in the Son Jesus. The working out of this "settlement in principle" still lies ahead of us. That is why we must assert that salvation remains an incomplete process in practice. But the revelation in the Incarnation coupled with the revelation of Sinai has given humankind the blueprint and the power to achieve full wholeness as individuals and as the basic community of the children of God.

The Christ event completed the process of stripping away the barriers to the full understanding of how the human community could assert its dignity and at the same time acknowledge its dependence on the Creator God. The fundamentally sinful condition of humankind could be overcome. The only qualification I would make to the traditional notion of Christ as Savior is that this salvific dimension must be seen as the culmination of the process begun with Sinai and not as a replacement for the Sinai experience. Without an understanding of the communal dimensions of reconciliation and the link between ultimate reconciliation and human history—the core of the Sinaitic revelation—the notion of Christ as Savior becomes truncated and in the last analysis significantly distorted.

A Summary

As we move to the conclusion of this chapter, it is necessary to reaffirm its tentativeness. It represents an attempt to rearrange the context of the Christian-Jewish discussion regarding Christology. All the contrasts presented here need refinement and further elaboration. Perhaps new research will render some of the suggested contrasts invalid. The articulation of a new definition of Christianity's role vis-à-vis Judaism will involve many years of theological reflection, for it touches upon the very self-identity of the Church.

To summarize the general orientation of my approach, it hinges around the following principles: (1) any Christology that simply presents the meaning of Jesus' ministry as the fulfillment of Jewish Messianic prophecies is invalid; (2) the basic link between Jesus and Judaism must be sought in his sharing of the revolutionary vision of Pharisaic Judaism; (3) the difference between Christianity and Judaism theologically—and the difference should not be papered over—is to be found in Christianity's acceptance of Incarnational Christology and its attendant notions; this Christology, however, involves a firm retention of Judaism's commitment to justice within history; (4) Judaism's principal contribution to Christological thought will come from understanding the Exodus covenantal tradition and the sense of salvation within history that this covenant entails as well as the sense of peoplehood; (5) Christian-Jewish dialogue on the Christological question has implications for the Church everywhere, and not only in the North Atlantic region of the world as some Christians have argued, for there is no way to understand Christology authentically without understanding the thoroughly Jewish context of Jesus' ministry; Christian understanding of Judaism becomes an imperative regardless of the presence or absence of Jews in a particular geographic area; (6) Christianity and Judaism will both have to prepare themselves to relate their covenantal theological tradition to other world religions and ideologies. The growing interdependence of the world community makes this a theological as well as an ethical imperative for both faith communities.

6
Christology in the Light
of the Auschwitz Experience

Anyone acquainted with recent directions in Jewish thought is well aware of the central role that the Nazi Holocaust has come to play. While major interpreters of the Auschwitz experience within present-day Judaism, such as Irving Greenberg, Emil Fackenheim, Henry Friedlander, Richard Rubenstein, Eliezer Berkovits and Elie Wiesel, may differ profoundly as to its ultimate significance, they all agree on its profound impact on Jewish self-identity in our time. Given the general goal of this volume—an examination of Christology in the context of the Christian-Jewish dialogue—the obvious question confronts us: Does the Holocaust in any way affect the contemporary formulation of Christology? For most of the major systematicians it has not played any role at all, even those working out of a German setting. Eva Fleischner rightly laments this fact.[201] Hans Küng speaks with admirable sensitivity about the sufferings of the Jews at the hands of the Nazis. But this concern has not yet penetrated his basic theological model. The Holocaust never rates even a mention in the Christological formulations offered by the liberation theologians.

A few Christian scholars have begun of late to wrestle with the Holocaust event, asking in what way the Church needs to adjust its theological vision in light of Auschwitz. The names here include Franklin Sherman, Marcel Dubois, Jürgen Moltmann, Gregory Baum, Douglas J. Hall and Clemens Thoma. I applaud these attempts even though I am not in full agreement with all of them. We shall examine their respective positions shortly.

Why the Holocaust Has an Impact on Christology

As a preface to our look at some concrete efforts at Christological expression in the post-Holocaust era, it would be important to state some working principles as to why the question of the Christology-Auschwitz connection must be asked by Christian theologians. The Holocaust was first of all, as the Church historian Franklin Littell has rightly insisted, an event in Christian history, as well as one in Jewish history. While I would subscribe to the position of historians like Uriel Tal that the Holocaust was in the last analysis the product of secular, profoundly anti-Christian forces and not simply the final chapter in the long history of Christian antisemitism, there is no doubt that traditional Christian antisemitism provided an indispensable seedbed for the successful implementation of the Nazi "Final Solution."[202]

But even beyond this link to Christianity, reflection on the Holocaust's significance for Christological understanding becomes crucial because of some of the general principles central to this volume: (1) that revelation remains open and ongoing; (2) that history is not yet fulfilled and that it remains a revelatory locus—hence a major event such as the Nazi Holocaust must be scrutinized for theological significance; (3) that Christian theology remains incomplete without the religious insights offered by the Jewish covenant—hence any event having a major impact on that covenant, as Auschwitz obviously has, by implication conditions theological thinking in the Church. Strictly dialogical considerations aside, the Holocaust experience must find its way into the articulation of basic Christian theological themes today, Christology notwithstanding.

Christology and Auschwitz: Some Systematic Perspectives

Among the major theological figures of this generation, Jürgen Moltmann has been the only one to attempt an exposition of Christology against the background of Auschwitz. As we have already seen briefly in Chapter 3, this concern is at the heart of his volume *The Crucified God.* Moltmann speaks of his own personal reactions to a postwar visit to the concentration camp at Maidanek in Poland:

> With each step it became physically more difficult to go further and look at the thousands of children's shoes, clothing remnants, collected hair, and gold teeth. At that moment I would have preferred from

shame to be swallowed up by the earth, if I had not believed: "God is
with them. They will rise again." Later, I found in the visitors' book the
inscriptions of others. "Never again can this be allowed to happen. We
will fight to see that this never again comes to pass." I respect this
answer, but it does not help the murdered ones. I also respect my own
answer, which I gave at that time. But it is not sufficient.[203]

Moltmann goes on to raise the question of how faith in God remains
possible after the Holocaust. The answer is profoundly difficult, but
Moltmann says that he has found some response in reflecting on a story
found in the novel *Night* by the Holocaust survivor Elie Wiesel. The story
ends with the words "Where is God? . . . He hangs there from the
gallows. . . ." So, for Moltmann, the experience of Auschwitz revealed
perhaps more dramatically than any event since the Crucifixion the basic
meaning of the Christ event—God can save people, including Israel,
because through the Cross he participated in their very suffering. To
theologize after Auschwitz would prove an impossibility in Moltmann's
view

> . . . were not the *Sch'ma* Israel and the Lord's Prayer prayed in Ausch-
> witz itself, were not God Himself in Auschwitz, suffering with the
> martyred and murdered. Every other answer would be blasphemy. An
> absolute God would make us indifferent. The God of action and success
> would let us forget the dead, which we still cannot forget. God as
> Nothingness would make the entire world into a concentration camp.[204]

Moltmann makes some linkage between his theology of the Cross and
its salvific effect even for the people Israel and Abraham Heschel's notion
of *divine pathos* which we briefly examined in the last chapter. He also
argues that the notion of the suffering of God as the basic divine salvific
activity is consonant with rabbinic theology of the first century:

> The God who suffers in exile with Israel preserves the people from
> despair and fear. The realization of God's fellow-suffering impedes
> apathy, maintains sympathy for God in life, and holds hope for the
> future of God open.[205]

Moltmann adds that in rabbinic theology it is claimed that this suffering
on the part of God is something he experiences at the very core of his
being. God is not merely present where people are suffering; that suffering

directly affects his own life. As Moltmann puts it, "God is not only involved in history; history is also in God himself."[206]

Placed in the context of the Incarnational Christology advocated in this volume, Moltmann seems to be saying that humanity and divinity touch most profoundly at the moment of human suffering. This was clearly seen in the Crucifixion. But the Resurrection showed that this linkage in suffering between humankind and its Creator leads finally to a new state of wholeness and unity, to final salvation, to ultimate reconciliation between creatures and their Creator God.

Moltmann's efforts at viewing Christology in the context of Auschwitz has met with mixed reactions from theologians connected with the dialogue. We have previously indicated some of the negative reactions of A. Roy Eckardt. He is strong and blunt in his rejection of Moltmann's theology of the Cross. There is no way we can honestly assert that the millions of Jews were *liberated* from death or from any other suffering through the Crucifixion. It approaches blasphemy to make such a claim in light of Christian complicity with the Nazi "Final Solution." He writes:

> What does it mean to tell the inmates of Buchenwald or Bergen-Belsen, as this Christian theologian does, that "through his suffering and death, the risen Christ brings righteousness and life to the unrighteousness and the dying"?[207]

For Eckardt, Moltmann simply claims too much for the sufferings of Christ. "It may be contended," Eckardt argues, "that in comparison with certain other sufferings, Jesus' death becomes relatively non-significant."[208] This is also a point made by Eugene Borowitz in his recent volume.[209]

Eckardy also feels that emphasizing the theology of the Cross leads to an overidealization of certain categories such as "weakness," "impotence," "vulnerability," "openness to suffering and love," and "divine protection." This religious outlook will only serve to expose all believers, and in a special way the Jews, to grave danger. For as both Irving Greenberg[210] and Richard Rubenstein[211] have insisted in somewhat different ways, the judicious use of power becomes a moral necessity in view of the evil exposed in Auschwitz. I shall make some assessment of Eckardt's critique later on in this chapter.

Another Christian theologian sensitive to the issue of the Christian-Jewish dialogue and Auschwitz in particular, Douglas J. Hall, sees Moltmann's efforts and the theology of the Cross generally in a much more sympathetic light than Eckardt. He is firm in maintaining that the development of the theology of the Cross is the only way to overcome the kind of Christological thinking which inevitably leads to the antisemitism manifested in the Holocaust. Only such theology in Hall's mind can counter the dangers inherent in "the historicizing of the eschatological" Christology which has dominated Christianity for so long a time and which Rosemary Ruether has so ably critiqued. Hall writes:

> To recover and devise a theology of the Cross indigenous to our own time and place means—as Moltmann has demonstrated so ably—to recover and devise a theology of hope. Only such a theology, which does not know everything in advance, "like the ant," but is always "properly astonished at events" (Barth), can function as a basis of dialogue and fraternity with other faiths—"the Jews first."[212]

A "theology of the Cross" Christology assumes the continuation of evil, sin and suffering after the Easter event. It completely rejects any claim that after the "victory of the third day" the human situation is no longer that of the Cross. This Christological approach establishes a soteriology of solidarity which by definition sets up the Cross of Jesus as a part of fraternal union with the Jewish people, and with all who seek human liberation and peace, not as a point of exclusion:

> ... the faith of Israel is incomprehensible unless one sees at its heart a suffering God whose solidarity with humanity is so abysmal that the "cross in the heart of God" (H. Wheeler Robinson) must always be incarnating itself in history. Reading the works of Elie Wiesel, one knows, as a Christian, that he bears this indelible resemblance to the people of Israel.[213]

For Hall, the theology of the Cross, of all available Christological options, expresses the thorough meaning of the Incarnation. It alone establishes the authentic divine-human link implied in the Word becoming flesh by emphasizing the solidarity of God himself with suffering humanity. Only the theology of the Cross offers a consistent and imaginative testimony to the genuine humanness of Jesus. As with Eckardt's position, some critique of Hall will be offered after the examination of additional viewpoints that move in the same direction.

One such perspective is found in the reflections of Franklin Sherman. He feels that Auschwitz has radically affected the possibilities of God-language. After the Holocaust the only legitimate theodicy is one that clearly acknowledges divine participation in the sufferings of people who in turn are summoned to take part in the sufferings of God. For Christianity, says Sherman,

> ... the symbol of the agonizing God is the cross of Christ. It is tragic that this symbol should have become a symbol of division between Jews and Christians, for the reality to which it points is a Jewish reality as well, the reality of suffering and martyrdom.[214]

For Sherman, the revelation of the cross is first and foremost the revelation of a fundamentally *Jewish* reality. Later theological reflection on the meaning of the Cross should not, and cannot, obscure this fundamental fact. Here Sherman argues in much the same manner as Moltmann, citing the works of Abraham Heschel: the Cross reveals the same divine participation in the sufferings of people that was already shown to us in the teachings of the prophets, particularly in Jeremiah. This understanding of the revelation of the Cross and its profound links with the Jewish prophetic tradition should make Christians the first to identify with the sufferings of the Jewish people, especially with their experience of Auschwitz. "We can speak of God after Auschwitz," Sherman writes, "only as the one who calls us to a new unity as between brothers—not only between Jews and Christians, but especially between Jews and Christians."[215]

Echoes of a similar perspective appear in the writings of the Israeli Christian Marcel Dubois. While deeply conscious of the difficulty Christians face in setting the reality of Auschwitz within the context of a theology of the Cross, and recognizing that such a linkage may appear as an obscenity to Jews whose sufferings in the Holocaust were in part due to the Church's moral failure, he nonetheless feels that this is the direction which Christological interpretation must take after the Holocaust:

> ... in the person of the Suffering Servant there appears to take place an ineffable change. Our vision of Jewish destiny and our understanding of the Holocaust in particular depend on our compassion; the Calvary of the Jewish people, whose summit is the Holocaust, can help us to understand a little better the mystery of the cross.[216]

Dubois is convinced that under the guidance of faith the Christian can truly affirm that Jesus fulfills Israel in her destiny of Suffering Servant and that Israel, in her experience of solitude and anguish, answers and represents even without knowing it the mystery of the Passion and the

Cross. The challenge of the massive human annihilation which the Holocaust era ushered in stands before both Jews and Christians:

> They have learnt to be united in compassion; they must now learn to be united in hope, the hope . . . of the people that believes in the victory of life and in the fidelity of God.[217]

Clemens Thoma has also posited some connections between Christology and the Holocaust, though only in a skeletal sort of way. He understands the Holocaust as rooted in an antisemitic ideology that was at root anti-Christian as well. Hence Christian guilt for Auschwitz cannot be preached indiscriminately. Yet, Thoma will clearly acknowledge that Christian hatred of the Jews greatly facilitated the "Final Solution." Speaking more theologically, his ideas bear a resemblance to those of Moltmann, Sherman and Dubois:

> . . . a believing Christian should not find it so very difficult to interpret the sacrifice of the Jews during the Nazi terror. His thoughts should be turned toward Christ to whom these Jewish masses became alike, in sorrow and death. Auschwitz is the most monumental sign of our time for the intimate bond and unity between the Jewish martyrs—who stand for all Jews—and the crucified Christ, even though the Jews in question could not be aware of it.[218]

Gregory Baum is the final theologian we shall briefly look at in this chapter. Unlike Moltmann, Hall, Sherman and Dubois, Baum does not explicitly link authentic post-Auschwitz Christology with the theology of the Cross. For him Auschwitz serves more as the destroyer of certain Christological trends rather than as a clear indication of the singular validity of the theology of the Cross:

> Auschwitz . . . is an altogether special sign of the times, in which God empowers the Church to correct its past teaching, *including its central dogma,* to the extent that it distorts God's action in Christ and promotes human destruction. . . . The Holocaust acted out the Church's fantasy that the Jews were a non-people, that they had no place before God and that they should have disappeared long ago by accepting Christ. The Church is now summoned to a radical reformulation of its faith, free of ideological deformation, making God's act in Christ fully and without reserve a message for life rather than death.[219]

However one states the Incarnational reality today, the Holocaust, as Baum sees it, has made it imperative to articulate it in such a way as to affirm the continuing validity of Judaism. In other words Christology must cease having antisemitism as its left hand.

An Evaluation of the Christology-Auschwitz Link

Some commentary on the above perspectives is now in order. To begin with, there is need to affirm without the slightest qualification that Auschwitz has made it immoral for Christians to maintain any Christology that is overly triumphalistic or that finds the significance of the Christ event in the elimination of the Jewish covenant. In this general emphasis all the above theologians are quite to the point. Likewise the viewpoint that in light of the Holocaust the fate of Jews and Christians has become inextricably linked is worthy of endorsement.

But from the fact that the Christological model outlined in the previous chapter does not make direct reference to the theology of the Cross it should be evident that my understanding is somewhat different. In the first place, I am bothered by the propriety of combining the theology of the Cross with the Auschwitz experience in light of significant Christian complicity in the Nazi effort. The Cross has always been described as a voluntary act on the part of God and his Son; the Cross can be understood in a redemptive fashion when seen as the culmination and the consequence of Jesus' active ministry. Auschwitz was neither voluntary nor redemptive in any sense. Here Emil Fackenheim's contention that to assign any form of *meaning* to the Holocaust is blasphemy must be safeguarded at all costs. Also, as was stressed in Chapter 4, the attempts by Moltmann and Sherman to tie the theology of the Cross to Heschel's notion of "divine pathos" disregards the difference that Heschel himself insisted upon between his view and the notion of the Incarnation.

The theology of the Cross is consistent with, and helpful for, the Incarnational Christology presented in Chapter 4 in at least one respect. Hence I feel that Eckardt's criticism of Moltmann is somewhat overdrawn. Insofar as this theology of the Cross reveals the vulnerability of God and his dependence on humanity, insofar as it forces upon us a new understanding of the God-human person relationship in which there is greater divine-human communion and interdependence both in creativity and in suffering, it definitely enhances the understanding of Christology that emerges from a study of Jesus' ministry within its Pharisaic setting. The theology of the Cross approach advocated by Douglas Hall without question resonates in important ways with central motifs in Incarnational Christology as I have tried to articulate it.

But I remain uneasy about making the Cross the central focus of Christology and the primary locus of the divine-human encounter. It may rob both Pharisaic Judaism and the Christ event of some of their inherent richness. Suffering must be recognized as a vital component of human living, but it is by no means the only one. Here the critique made by Francis Fiorenza is very much to the point:

> ... my emphasis on the Resurrection (against Moltmann) can be seen historically as an attempt to reclaim for systematic theology the so-called classic idea of atonement over contemporary emphases of a theology of the cross. The classic idea views the life of Jesus as a whole and conceives of atonement in terms of conflict and victory. The work and person of Jesus are seen as one. Atonement and redemption, reconciliation and salvation are seen in their fundamental unity.[220]

Fiorenza goes on to add that in the classic perspective the work of Christ is seen in terms of victory over the powers holding humankind in bondage, sin and death. Sin is not interpreted in an exclusively individualistic sense nor as a fundamental cleavage between a higher and a lower self. Rather this theology uplifts the social dimensions of sin. Sin is understood as an objective power keeping men and women in bondage. It basically involves a lack of fellowship with God, the end result being death. Christ's ministry and death on the cross overcame this by recreating fellowship between humankind and God.

While Fiorenza's viewpoint bears some of the same limitations vis-à-vis the Jewish context of Jesus' ministry common to liberation theologians, his emphasis on the significance of the whole of Jesus' ministry needs to be part of any authentic Christology. Overemphasis on the Cross will lead to distortion.

Eckardt's criticism of Moltmann's version of the theology of the Cross on the question of power is well stated. The Christology presented in Chapter 4, with its stress on Jesus' active revolutionary stance as part of the Pharisaic movement, would be uneasy with Moltmann's emphasis on the "weakness" of the Cross. This Christology exhibits a far greater sympathy for the basic thrust of liberation theology than Moltmann would allow. In so doing it is much closer to the authentic Jewish tradition, despite Moltmann's attempt to link his theology of the Cross approach to

Heschel's understanding of divine pathos in the prophetic tradition. While there is need for dialogue on the power question with Jewish Holocaust interpreters such as Irving Greenberg and Richard Rubenstein—and the moral traditions of Christianity may have some definite contributions to make to this dialogue—using a Moltmann-type "theology of the Cross" Christology as the exclusive starting point will not prove productive for Christian-Jewish conversation. Hall's approach to the question would be somewhat different from Moltmann's. I suspect that his feelings toward the Christological outlook of the liberationists would be far more positive, but Hall needs to elaborate his position much more fully in this regard.

The Holocaust and the Problem of Evil

One issue that the Holocaust raises for theology generally, but especially for the relatively "optimistic" approach to Christology presented in the preceding chapter, is that of evil. A. Roy Eckardt seems to say that when all is said and done the only way to understand the shattering event that was Auschwitz is by attributing it to the work of the devil. This follows from his general contention that all antisemitism is ultimately demonic in origin:

> ... the "devil" and "anti-Semitism" are correlative realities: anti-Semitism is born of the devil, and the devil receives his sustenance from anti-Semitism. The elucidation or disclosure of the devil is required etiologically and existentially because the hatred of Jews is not, in essence, a matter of evil as such, but is *this* evil, an evil absolutely incomparable and absolutely incredible (just as the choice of the Jews by God is absolutely incredible, the one totally unique act of salvation in this world).[221]

Eckardt is quite correct that the massive and grotesque scale of evil unleashed in the Holocaust rules out any simplistic explanation of its origins. Yet, locating the genesis of evil outside of humanity fails to deal with the problem in its ultimate depths. To place the root of the evil that Auschwitz represents outside of the human person constitutes an "easy" solution—it leaves the dignity of the human person pretty much unscathed. It is more accurate in my perspective to understand the evil perpetrated by the Nazis as ultimately the product of forces at work within human consciousness since the time of human creation.

The act of creation constituted the liberation of humanity from its total encasement in the Godhead. The Creator God recognized that he had to let go of part of himself in order to develop and become fully God. He thus granted the newly made humankind the powers of co-creatorship. But that part of God's humanity that now took on an independent existence was forced to work out a new relationship with the Godhead; at times it even tried to supplant the Godhead. For centuries, fear largely kept such desire in check. But with the dawning of the modern age the human community began to experience a new sense of freedom, a widespread Prometheus-Unbound experience, and to lose the once overpowering fear of the Creator God. Since the problem of the new relationship between God and humanity had not been adequately developed as yet and since the temptation to try to overcome God still lingered within humanity, the new liberation of humanity opened the doors to catastrophe. That catastrophe saw realization in the Holocaust. As the Israeli historian Uriel Tal has strongly insisted, there was a total reversal of meanings in Nazism in which the human person finally tried to subdue the Creator.[222]

It is vitally important to try to define the root cause of the evil that was Auschwitz, for without such knowledge we will remain powerless to prevent its recurrence. A devil-origins theory makes it almost impossible to sustain any hope of preventing another outbreak of such an event. However, by understanding this evil as rooted in the centuries-long struggle of the human community to define its proper relationship to the Creator, one is at least provided with some possibility of accomplishing this goal. The final assertion of human freedom from God in our time may in fact be the beginning of the ultimate resolution of the conflict. The human community is beginning to understand, to more fully appreciate, the dimensions of co-creatorship that God has bestowed upon men and women. The "Abba" dimensions of the God-human person relationship are becoming clearer. The fear and the paternalism that characterized the relationship in the past are coming to an end. The revolution begun by the Pharisees and Jesus is coming closer to realization.

Evil will be redeemed and conquered only when humankind develops, along with a sense of dignity and a new grasp of the powers it possesses to shape itself and its environment, a sense of profound humility evoked by the experience of the healing power present in the ultimate Creator of this human power. This experience has been made possible through the Pharisaic-Jesus revolution. Only the integration of this awareness into mass consciousness will finally overcome evil and neutralize attempts such as the Holocaust for humanity to "elevate" itself above the Creator. This intimate personal healing must also be tied, for full wholeness and salvation, to the sense of communal interdependence revealed by the Sinai covenant. Hence the Incarnational Christology outlined in this volume, when coupled with the unique salvific elements found in Judaism, represents the ultimate answer to the challenge of the Holocaust. Saying this in no way lessens the tragedy nor fails to appreciate the depth of suffering experienced by its victims. But in the final analysis and after much soul-searching I stand ready to claim that the Holocaust has not undercut the deepest meaning of Christology as presented in this volume, especially when that Christology is placed, as it must be, within its Jewish setting.

The Holocaust has unquestionably shattered many conventional Christological claims. It has rendered any Christological approach that rejects Jews and Judaism as religious relics a moral obscenity. That is why theologians like Eckardt and Ruether must be given a serious hearing. It also forces us to appreciate more intensely God's dependence on the human community—something implied in the "Abba" experience of God. And "optimistic" theologians such as the liberationists need to treat much more seriously demonic events like Auschwitz.[223]

But the core meaning of Christology remains despite the Holocaust. In fact it is my contention that this core meaning has become even more urgent in light of Auschwitz which increasingly we are coming to appreciate not merely as an isolated period in modern history but as marking the beginning of a new era—one in which the combination of technology, bureaucracy and moral passivity have combined to make possible human destruction on an unprecedented scale.

7

Christian Mission
and the Jewish People

The approach to Christology outlined in the previous chapters raises at least two further questions that need some attention: (1) the mission to the Jews; (2) the depiction of Jews in the Christian liturgy. We can only touch upon them here. Both require further reflection and discussion among Christian scholars because they impinge upon the core of Christian belief and proclamation.

Regarding the question of the mission to the Jews, a growing body of literature has developed over the past several years. At times the discussion has been intense, more so within Protestantism than Catholicism. The greater interest in the issue among Protestant Christians may be due to the continued presence in their midst of official organizations for proselytizing Jews, unlike Roman Catholicism where since Vatican Council II the still extant groups have dramatically changed their *raison d'être* from mission to dialogue. An additional source of greater Protestant interest in the question may be due to its more focused attention on the biblical tradition as the exclusive source of revelation and theological meaning. But even in Catholic circles, as is evident from some of the reactions to the previously cited recent study document by Tomaso Federici of the San Anselmo Pontifical Faculty in Rome, the issue is far from resolved. While I am not fully acquainted with the scene in Orthodox Christianity, I suspect that its general orientation on the Jewish question would lead the theological majority in the tradition to maintain some sort of Christian obligation to make Christ known to the Jewish people.

One example of the passion that the mission issue can elicit is to be found in a series of responses to an article by a leading Jewish ecumenical figure, Balfour Brickner. In his piece referred to in Chapter 1, Brickner urged his Christian colleagues to formally renounce any goal of proselytizing Jews. Among those who responded to his call—all members of Protestant churches—there emerged an unyielding belief that acquiescence to Brickner's request would prove impossible. It would involve Christians, in the mind of the respondents, in a fundamental act of unfaithfulness. They would be guilty of abandoning the Gospel mandate to preach the good news to all men and women.[224]

In a response to the Federici paper, George P. Graham, ecumenical officer for the Rockville Center diocese in New York, argues in a similar vein from inside the Catholic tradition. The Federici approach is inadequate in his mind because it fails to present a position on mission and witness in the context of the more fundamental Catholic teachings about the nature of the Church.[225] Graham feels that Vatican Council II emphasized the indispensability of the Church for salvation. While Graham does not rule out salvation outside the Church, he does insist that anyone who knows that the Church was made necessary by God through Christ and refuses to enter it stands to be rejected by the Lord. Hence he maintains that the Church has a solemn obligation to preach the message of Christ to the whole world. Federici, he believes, has clouded the issue.

We shall examine Federici's basic position in a moment. Before doing so, however, it is necessary to state clearly the conviction that the Christological understanding prevailing in the previous pages demands a thorough rethinking of traditional Christian notions about proselytism and the Jews. This is ultimately rooted in the belief, spelled out in some detail in the previous chapters, that Judaism has preserved aspects of the full biblical revelation better than Christianity. Christians need to talk with Jews to recover this lost understanding. This is especially crucial relative to the significance of Jesus' teachings and person which have frequently been misinterpreted because they have been disconnected from their Jewish context. Understanding the Jewish-Christian situation in this manner, it will not prove possible to approach Jews in the haughty ways usually associated with Christian mission. Christians are not in a position to simply offer Christ as the means to salvation. They must also acknowledge their own salvific nakedness and stand ready to learn from the Jewish tradition, even to learn more about what Jesus was saying and doing in his time.

Such an approach, let me make clear, rests on three working principles. The first is the recognition that Christianity and the Gospel of Jesus cannot be understood apart from their deep immersion in Judaism—a fact that the Church has usually forgotten for most of its long history. Recovery of this awareness will inevitably modify Christianity's customary superiority complex vis-à-vis Judaism. Second, it relies heavily on the notion, briefly alluded to in Chapter 1, that revelation remains an ongoing process. Hence we can never take the New Testament's view on the question of the Church's relationship to the Jews as the last word. And third, while I would agree with scholars such as Gregory Baum[226] that St. Paul's well-known reflections on the Christian-Jewish relationship in Romans 9—11 are inadequate as they stand, I do think that they help to support my second principle. Rather than taking the model offered by St. Paul in these chapters as the definitive word on the subject, we should rather adopt the *spirit* of Romans 9—11, namely that even at the end of his ministerial career Paul had not been able to fully resolve for himself the proper way to describe the ongoing relationship between Christians and Jews. After many years of thought Paul had come to the conclusion that while still a mystery for him, the relationship was one marked by profound continuity. Rather than simply stopping at the precise formulation of Romans 9—11, the Church today needs to continue Paul's agonizing search into this question.

The Christological rethinking presented earlier is one attempt to take up the Pauline challenge. Thus my theological methodology differs significantly from that advocated, e.g., by Graham. Although Federici is somewhat more cautious and less explicit than I am, I feel that he is moving in the same direction that I am. There is little doubt that the question of Christian mission to the Jews depends quite heavily and directly on one's hermeneutical stance. Basic differences here will undoubtedly bring about differences on the mission question. There is no use in pretending that this is not the case. The disagreements among Christian scholars regarding proselytizing go well beyond the issue itself. Ultimately they represent a specification of a chosen theological stance. And there is no way of resolving the tension on this point without facing the more basic methodological question.

To return to the Federici paper, in my judgment it represents one of the most important recent statements on the topic. This is in part due to the context in which it was originally presented: a March 1977 meeting in Venice of the Vatican-Jewish international liaison committees. While in no sense an official Vatican statement, it was cleared with important sectors of the Vatican. Hence it represents more than just an ordinary theological presentation by an individual scholar. Important sources in the Vatican were at least open to this kind of rethinking of the mission question suggested by Federici.

Basic to Federici is a distinction between proselytism and witness—and *witness* he understands very much in a dialogic sense. There admittedly remains some ambiguity on this point in Federici's position. One senses that he would like to go further than the official Vatican context of his presentation will allow. He does not *clearly* reject proselytism as such but has added the qualifying adjective *undue.* He likewise reaffirms the need for the Church to announce and carry out its mission of universal proclamation of the Gospel.

Included under Federici's proposed ban are all forms of preaching or witness which in any manner constrain individual Jews, or the Jewish community as a whole, whether that constraint be of the physical, moral, psychological or cultural variety. He goes on to exclude as well

> ... every kind of disqualifying judgment, contempt or prejudice that could be levelled against the Jewish people or individual Jews as such, or against their faith, their worship, their culture in general and their religious culture in particular; against their past and present history, their existence and the meaning of their existence. Excluded also are odious types of discussion, especially those harmful forms ... which try to exalt the Christian religion or Christianity as such by discrediting Jewish religion and Judaism, whether past or present.[227]

Yet, despite the remaining murkiness in Federici's section on proselytism, the third part of his essay strongly emphasizes the need for witness to take place in a setting of reverent dialogue. Such dialogue, if it is to be sincere,

> ... demands authentic self-discipline. Every temptation to exclusivism must be eliminated as also any imperialism or self-sufficiency. On the other hand there must be fidelity and dedicated personal searching, avoiding any form of relativism and syncretism that would try artificially to combine irreconcilable elements. Once the spiritual identity of the one and the other is guaranteed, there must be mutual esteem and respect (theological as well), and the conviction that every growth and bettering in the spiritual field comes about with the other's contribution.[228]

It should be obvious from the spirit inherent in the above quotation that Federici is rejecting without qualification all conventional missionary approaches toward the Jewish people. Such efforts, marked as they have been by a sense of superiority in faith on the part of Christians, must be totally eliminated. Those of us who join Federici in this call in no way mean to imply that dialogue is a new missionary technique. Rather it constitutes a recognition on the part of Christians that while they have important contributions to make to humanity's religious understanding, their own faith needs to be deepened and expanded by loving contact with the faith of all non-Christians, but in a special way with the Jewish tradition which, as has been shown above, is central to a proper understanding of Jesus' ministry, Christology and the mandate of the Church.

In the course of the dialogue which has been purged of all notions of superiority and all forms of proselytizing, Christians will try to convey to Jews why they feel that the Christ event carries a central meaning for the entire human family. Here Federici is rejecting the position advocated by such theologians as Paul Van Buren which, as was shown in Chapter 2, would see Christian identity as nothing more than Judaism for the Gentiles. I think Federici is correct in such a rejection. As this volume has indicated on several occasions, unless some specific, unique and central content is preserved with respect to the Christ event, Christianity has very little reason to remain a separate world religion.

Since the new relationship between Christians and Jews is dialogic in nature, Christians will be eager to listen to explanations of the central insights of the Jewish faith tradition; they will try to understand the unique dimensions of the Jewish faith perspective, outlined in Chapter 5, and how and whether these may be authentically appropriated to Christian faith expression.

If a criticism can be made of Federici it is that he does not go far enough. He fails to really break with all aspects of the "total fulfillment" interpretation of Christology which has been responsible for Christian theology's destructive superiority complex vis-à-vis Judaism and other non-Christian religions throughout the centuries. I am convinced that this attitude must be clearly repudiated if Christian theology is to become ecumenical at its core. The contemporary call for the cessation of Christian missionary efforts toward Jews, which Federici has joined, will assume theological validity only if it is linked to current Christological reinterpretation within the Church, along the lines previously outlined in this volume. Failing this, such a position will continue to look to many like a failure in carrying out the supposed Gospel mandate to preach the good news to all nations.

The approach to witness advocated by Federici, it should be noted, appears to stand in harmony with the Jewish sense of witness obligation. This point is made by Leon Klenicki in commenting on the Federici paper.

Quoting Isaiah 43:10—"You are witnesses, says the Lord"—Klenicki speaks of Israel's vocation to witness to the world:

> The call of Israel is to stand among the peoples of the world as an image of sanctity, *Kedushah,* reflecting the inner being of God. . . . Sanctification of the Name is a process of daily vital commitment covering every aspect of the individual existence. . . . This [personal and communal] witnessing has meant through the centuries the offering of lives, the sacrifice of whole communities in defense of an eternal covenant.[229]

Insofar as the Christology presented above has tried to maintain distinct but ultimately complementary roles for Judaism and Christianity, the possibility of witness by each tradition, rather than serving as a source of division, can become a source of mutual strength and cooperation. Both Judaism and Christianity need to approach the question of witness as equally "givers" and "receivers."

We also need to be sensitive to the sense of mission as service. This is a point especially highlighted by Gregory Baum.[230] Such witness is all the more necessary in light of the experience of the Holocaust. Irving Greenberg has rightly called it an "orienting event" for both Christians and Jews in our day. Greenberg insists that the only way Jews and Christians can give faith witness to each other and to the world is by acts of life affirmation. Thus if Christians want to share with Jews their insights about the Incarnation it is imperative that they undertake actions which concretely support life throughout the world. The revolutionary impulse inherent in the reformulated Christology offered in Chapter 4 clearly demands such life-affirming "missionary" witness on the part of Christians, and in particular toward the Jewish community who have for so long suffered because of Christian antisemitism.

Two final points. The above remarks have concentrated on the notion of mission as an overall theological policy in the Church. A close examination of the Federici paper will show that he does not exclude the possibility that in the course of witness in dialogue an individual may decide that he or she can achieve an intensification of the spiritual life by transferring from one faith community to the other. It is impossible to factor out such a possibility *a priori.* But conversion can never be set forth as the direct aim of dialogical witness. Acknowledging the incompleteness of all present faith traditions, Judaism and Christianity included, personal decisions about conversion must be left to the judgment of the individual person and ultimately to the mystery of God's grace.

Finally, the incorporation of a new theology of mission, rooted in the reformulated Christology presented in this volume, into the consciousness of the Christian faithful will only come about if we are willing to significantly revamp parts of our liturgy. This of course applies most directly to those Christian communities with a sacramental tradition. A good deal of discussion has taken place in the dialogue about such specific issues as liturgical readings in which the Jews appear in a negative light and the Holy Week liturgy. Some of the problems have already been corrected or steps in that direction are under way. All this is important and necessary, but the problem is much deeper. So much of current liturgy, especially during the key periods of Lent and Advent, revolves around the notion of Jesus as fulfilling the biblical promises about the Messiah and the Messianic age. Yet we have seen how any number of theologians are rejecting the simplistic prophecy-fulfillment Christology. Unless we address this difficult and pivotal problem, our reformulated Christology will remain in the realm of pure theory with little effect on the average Christian's attitude toward the missionizing of Jews. It is a momumental and difficult task, one that will require much cooperation among liturgists, theologians, Scripture scholars and Church leaders. But, in the light of Auschwitz, it is one that can no longer wait. The life-affirmation witness that Greenberg and Baum have called for demands that we launch this effort as soon as possible.

Notes

1. Most of the relevant documents have been compiled by Helga Croner, *Stepping Stones to Further Jewish-Christian Relations* (New York: Stimulus Books, 1977).

2. Cf. the articles in the special issue of the *Journal of Ecumenical Studies* 13, No. 4 (Fall 1976). Also, Thomas Hopko, "Response to John Pawlikowski," in *Auschwitz: Beginning of a New Era?* Eva Fleischner, ed. (New York: KTAV, The Cathedral of St. John the Divine, Anti-Defamation League of B'nai B'rith, 1977), pp. 191–197; and "Greek Orthodox View of the Dialogue," in *Christian Attitudes on Jews and Judaism* 63 (Dec. 1978), pp. 11–12. For Evangelical viewpoints cf. *Evangelicals and Jews in Conversation,* A. James Rudin, Marc H. Tannenbaum, Marvin R. Wilson, eds. (Grand Rapids: Baker, 1978).

3. The original study of Protestant materials was reported by Bernhard Olson, *Faith and Prejudice* (New Haven: Yale University Press, 1963). The material is updated in Gerald Strober, *Portrait of the Elder Brother* (New York: American Jewish Committee, National Conference of Christians and Jews, 1972). For commentary, cf. Franklin H. Littell, "The Strober Report," in *Journal of Ecumenical Studies* 9 (Fall 1972), pp. 860–862. On the Catholic side I have analyzed the results of the initial Catholic textbook studies at St. Louis University, in *Catechetics and Prejudice* (New York: Paulist Press, 1973). This was updated by Eugene Fisher, *Faith Without Prejudice* (New York: Paulist Press, 1977). The study of French, Spanish and Italian Catholic materials is reported by Claire Huchet Bishop, *How Catholics Look at Jews* (New York: Paulist Press, 1974).

4. *A Liturgical Interpretation of Our Lord's Passion in Narrative Form* (New York: National Conference of Christians and Jews, 1977), Israel Study Group Occasional Papers #1.

5. More material on the liturgical issue can be found in my essay "Judaism in Christian Education and Liturgy," in *Auschwitz,* Eva Fleischner, ed. (see note 2), pp. 155–178. Model Holocaust liturgies are available in Franklin Littell, *The Crucifixion of the Jews* (New York: Harper & Row, 1975), pp. 141–153; Donald W. McEvoy, *A Christian Service of Holocaust Remembrance-Yom Ha Shoah* (New York: National Conference of Christians and Jews, 1978), and Josephine Knopp, *Liturgies* (Philadelphia: National Institute on the Holocaust, 1978).

6. For a summary of the results and some updating, cf. *Highlights of Proceedings of the National Conference on Faith without Prejudice: Religion and the Teaching of Human Relations* (New York: American Jewish Committee, 1975).

7. Cf. Pinchas Lapide, "Jesus in Israeli Textbooks," in *Journal of Ecumenical Studies* 10 (Summer 1973), pp. 515–531.

8. Rosemary Ruether, *Faith and Fratricide* (New York: Seabury Press, 1974).

9. Balfour Brickner, "Christian Missionaries and a Jewish Response," in *Worldview* 21 (May 1978), pp. 37–41.

10. "Christians Challenge the Rabbi's Response," in *Worldview* 21 (July/August 1978), pp. 42–46.

11. The authorized translation of the Federici paper can be found in *Origins* (National Catholic Documentary Service) 8 (October 19, 1978); also in *Encounter Today* 13 (Winter/Spring 1978), pp. 18–36. An earlier translation (with additional essays on Christian mission) is available in *Face to Face,* an Interreligious Bulletin (Anti-Defamation League of B'nai B'rith) 3/4 (Fall/Winter, 1977).

12. Cf. Irving Greenberg, "Cloud of Smoke, Pillar of Fire: Judaism, Christianity, and Modernity after the Holocaust," in *Auschwitz,* Eva Fleischner, ed. (see note 2), pp. 20–52.

13. Charlotte Klein, *Anti-Judaism in Christian Theology* (Philadelphia: Fortress Press, 1978).

14. Peter Chirico, "Christian and Jew Today from a Christian Theological Perspective," in *Journal of Ecumenical Studies* 7 (Fall 1970), pp. 748–749.

15. Robert Schreiter, "Christology in the Jewish-Christian Encounter: An Essay-Review of Edward Schillebeeckx's *Jesuz het Verhaal van een Levende,*" in *Journal of the American Academy of Religion* 44 (December 1976), pp. 702–703.

16. Shemaryahu Talmon, "Towards World Community: Resources for Living Together—A Jewish View," in *The Ecumenical Review* 26 (October 1974), pp. 617–618. A perspective in a similar vein is offered by Henry Siegman, "A Decade of Catholic-Jewish Relations: A Reassessment," in *Journal of Ecumenical Studies* 15 (Spring 1978), pp. 243–260; and "Jews and Christians—Beyond Brotherhood Week," in *Worldview* 18 (December 1975), pp. 31–36.

17. Cf. Kurt Hruby, "Israel, Peuple de Dieu, Existe-t-il une Théologie d'Israel dans l'Eglise?" in *Lumière et Vie* 18 (March/April 1979); Jacques Maritain, *Redeeming the Time* (London: Centenary Press, 1943); Jean Daniélou and A. Chouraqui, *The Jews: Views and Counterviews* (New York: Newman Press, 1967); Augustin Cardinal Bea, *The Church and the Jewish People* (New York: Harper & Row, 1966).

18. Charles Journet, "The Mysterious Destinies of Israel," in *The Bridge,* Vol. II, John Oesterreicher, ed. (New York: Pantheon Books, 1956), pp. 35–90.

19. Jean Daniélou, *Dialogue with Israel* (Baltimore: Helicon Press, 1966); Jean Daniélou and André Chouraqui, *The Jews* (see note 17); *idem, The Theology of Jewish Christianity* (Chicago: Henry Regnery, 1964).

20. Hans Urs von Balthasar, *Church and World* (New York: Herder and Herder, 1967).

21. Augustin Cardinal Bea, *The Church and the Jewish People* (London: Geoffrey Chapman, 1966).

22. The continuity/discontinuity contrast has been employed by A. Roy Eckardt in *Elder and Younger Brothers* (New York: Schocken, 1973) and in Michael B. McGarry, *Christology after Auschwitz* (New York: Paulist Press, 1977).

23. Monika Hellwig, "Christian Theology and the Covenant of Israel," in *Journal of Ecumenical Studies* 7 (Winter 1970), pp. 37–51, and "Why We Still Can't Talk," in *Jewish-Christian Relations,* Robert Heyer, ed. (New York: Paulist Press, 1974), pp. 26–31; also "Bible Interpretation: Has Anything Changed?" in *Biblical Studies: Meeting Ground of Jews and Christians,* Lawrence Boadt, Helga Croner, Leon Klenicki, eds. (New York: Paulist Press, 1980, A Stimulus Book), pp. 172–179.

24. Monika Hellwig, "Christian Theology" (see note 23), p. 49.

25. *Ibid.*

26. Paul van Buren, *The Burden of Freedom* (New York: Seabury Press, 1976).

27. Cf. Arthur Cohen, "The Myth of the Judaeo-Christian Tradition," in *Commentary* 48 (November 1969), pp. 73–77, and Hans Jonas, "Judaism, Christianity and the Western Tradition," in *Commentary* 44 (November 1967), pp. 61–70.

28. Paul van Buren, *op.cit.,* pp. 97–98.

29. *Idem, Discerning the Way* (New York: Seabury Press, 1980). Cf. also *idem,* "Christ of the Church, not the Messiah of Israel," paper presented to the American Academy of Religion Convention, San Francisco, December 1977; also "Affirmation of the Jewish People: A Condition of Theological Coherence," in *Journal of the American Academy of Religion* (Supplement) 45 (September 1977), pp. 1035–1100.

30. Martin Hengel, *The Son of God* (Philadelphia: Fortress Press, 1978).

31. Paul van Buren, "Christ of the Church" (see note 29), pp. 15–16.

32. *Ibid.,* p. 16.

33. A. Roy Eckardt, *Elder and Younger Brothers* (see note 22), p. 142.

34. *Idem,* "A Response to Rabbi Olan," in *Religion in Life* 42 (Fall 1973), p. 409.

35. *Idem,* "1948 and 1974: Trembling Journey through the Covenant," paper presented to the Israel Study Group, Washington, D.C., October 25, 1974, p. 44.

36. *Idem,* "The Resurrection and the Holocaust," paper presented to the Israel Study Group, New York City, March 4, 1978, p. 13.

37. J. Coos Schoneveld, "Israel and the Church in Face of God: A Protestant Point of View," in *Immanuel* 3 (Winter 1973/74), pp. 80–83, and "The Re-

thinking of the Christian Relationship to the Jewish People—A Balance Sheet after Ten Years in Israel," paper delivered at the European Regional Conference on the Church and Judaism, Ede, Holland, February 14, 1978.

38. *Idem,* "The Re-thinking" (see note 37), p. 5.

39. James Parkes, *Judaism and Christianity* (Chicago: University of Chicago Press, 1948), p. 30.

40. *Idem, The Foundations of Judaism and Christianity* (London: Vallentine-Mitchell, 1960), p. 131.

41. *Idem, Prelude to Dialogue* (London: Vallentine-Mitchell, 1969), pp. 188–301. For a further discussion of Parkes' theology, cf. my essay "The Church and Judaism: The Thought of James Parkes," in *Journal of Ecumenical Studies* 6 (Fall 1969), pp. 573–597.

42. J. Coert Rylaarsdam, "Jewish-Christian Relationship: The Two Covenants and the Dilemmas of Christology," in *Journal of Ecumenical Studies* 9 (Spring 1972), p. 251.

43. Gregory Baum's principal statement on the issue can be found in the following essays: "The Jews, Faith and Ideology," in *The Ecumenist* 10 (1971/72), pp. 71–76; "The Doctrinal Basis for Jewish-Christian Dialogue," in *The Month* 224 (1967), pp. 232–245; "Introduction" to Rosemary Ruether's *Faith and Fratricide* (see note 8); and "Rethinking the Church's Mission after Auschwitz," in *Auschwitz,* Eva Fleischner, ed. (see note 2), pp. 113–128.

44. Gregory Baum, "Rethinking the Church's Mission" (see note 43), p. 127.

45. Michael McGarry, *Christology after Auschwitz* (see note 22), p. 83.

46. Rosemary Ruether, "An Invitation to Jewish-Christian Dialogue: In What Sense Can We Say That Jesus Was 'The Christ'?" in *The Ecumenist* 10 (January /February 1972), p. 17.

47. *Idem,* "Christian-Jewish Dialogue: New Interpretations," in *ADL Bulletin* 30 (May 1973), p. 4.

48. *Idem, Faith and Fratricide* (see note 8), pp. 247–248.

49. *Ibid.,* pp. 250–251.

50. Michael McGarry, *Christology after Auschwitz* (see note 22), pp. 87–91.

51. E. P. Sanders, *Paul and Palestinian Judaism* (Philadelphia: Fortress Press, 1977).

52. *Ibid.,* p. 548.

53. *Ibid.,* p. 549.

54. Clemens Thoma, *A Christian Theology of Judaism* (New York: Paulist Press, 1980, A Stimulus Book).

55. Hubert Frankemolle, "Jewish and Christian Messianism," in *Theology Digest* 28 (Fall 1980), p. 234.

56. Clemens Thoma, *op. cit.,* p. 66; cf. also p. 143.

57. *Ibid.,* pp. 13–14.

58. *Ibid.,* p. 127.

59. *Ibid.,* p. 114; cf. also p. 113.

60. *Ibid.,* p. 58.

61. Eva Fleischner, *Judaism in German Christian Theology Since 1945: Christianity and Israel Considered in Terms of Mission* (Metuchen, N.J.: Scarecrow Press, 1975).

62. Wolfhart Pannenberg, *Jesus: God and Man* (Philadelphia: Westminster Press, 1968).

63. *Ibid.,* pp. 253–254.

64. *Ibid.,* p. 255.

65. *Ibid.,* p. 269.

66. Richard John Neuhaus, "Introduction" to Wolfhart Pannenberg, *Theology and the Kingdom of God* (Philadelphia: Westminster Press, 1969), pp. 35–36.

67. Eugene Borowitz, "Anti-Semitism and the Christologies of Barth, Berkouwer and Pannenberg," in *Dialogue* 16 (Winter 1977), p. 40.

68. Hans Joachim Schoeps, *The Jewish-Christian Argument* (New York: Holt, Rinehart & Winston, 1963).

69. Cf. Wolfhart Pannenberg, *Theology and the Kingdom* (see note 66), p. 36.

70. *Idem, The Apostles' Creed in the Light of Today's Questions* (Philadelphia: Westminster Press, 1972).

71. *Ibid.,* p. viii.

72. Cf. Eugene Borowitz, *Contemporary Christologies, A Jewish Response* (New York: Paulist Press, 1980), pp. 181–182.

73. As an example of this, Rabbi Borowitz reports that at a discussion of Pannenberg and Judaism at the 1974 American Theological Society convention, no one seemed aware of the change of perspective found in his later writings; cf. "Antisemitism" (see note 67), p. 41.

74. Jürgen Moltmann, *The Crucified God* (New York: Harper & Row, 1974), p. 32.

75. *Ibid.,* p. 34.

76. *Ibid.,* p. 178.

77. *Idem, The Church in the Power of the Spirit: A Contribution to Messianic Ecclesiology* (New York: Harper & Row, 1977).

78. Cf. Eugene Borowitz, *Contemporary Christologies* (see note 72), pp. 87–88.

79. A. Roy Eckardt, "Jürgen Moltmann, the Jewish People, and the Holocaust," in *Journal of the American Academy of Religion* 44 (December 1976), p. 682.

80. *Ibid.,* p. 689.

81. *Ibid.,* p. 686.

82. Hans Küng, *On Being a Christian* (Garden City, N.Y.: Doubleday, 1976).

83. *Ibid.,* p. 167.

84. *Ibid.,* p. 174.

85. Cf. Hans Küng, Pinchas Lapide, "Is Jesus a Bond or Barrier? A Jewish-Christian Dialogue," in *Journal of Ecumenical Studies* 14 (Summer 1977), pp. 466–483. This dialogue also appears in Küng's volume, *Signposts for the Future* (New York: Doubleday, 1977).

86. Hans Küng, *On Being a Christian* (see note 82), p. 408.

87. *Ibid.,* p. 544.

88. *Ibid.,* p. 545.

89. Gregory Baum, "Küng and Kasper on Christ," in *The Ecumenist* 14 (January/February 1977), p. 20.

90. Edward Schillebeeckx, *Jesus: An Experiment in Christology* (New York: Seabury Press, 1979). The second volume of Schillebeeckx's Christology, *Christ: The Christian Experience and the Modern Man* (New York: Seabury Press, 1980), has appeared since the completion of this chapter. It touches upon Judaism, but nothing in it requires a major reassessment of what has been stated here.

91. *Idem, Jesus* (see note 90), p. 237.

92. *Ibid.,* p. 241.

93. *Ibid.,* p. 514.

94. *Ibid.,* p. 266.

95. *Ibid.,* p. 268.

96. Robert Schreiter, "Christology" (see note 15), p. 702.

97. Gustavo Gutierrez, *A Theology of Liberation* (Maryknoll: Orbis Books, 1973).

98. *Ibid.,* p. 156.

99. *Ibid.,* p. 158.

100. *Ibid.,* p. 161.

101. *Ibid.,* p. 256.

102. *Ibid.,* p. 231.

103. Leon Klenicki, "A Report on the Puebla Meeting of the Latin American Bishops' Conference (CELAM), January 27–February 13, 1979," in *ADL Memorandum* (New York: Anti-Defamation League, March 14, 1979), p. 7.

104. José Miguez Bonino, *Revolutionary Theology Comes of Age* (London: SPCK, 1975); the American edition is entitled *Doing Theology in a Revolutionary Situation* (Philadelphia: Fortress Press, 1975).

105. *Ibid.,* p. 77.

106. *Ibid.,* p. 165.

107. *Ibid.,* p. 166.

108. *Ibid.,* pp. 166–167.

109. Jon Sobrino, *Christology at the Crossroads* (Maryknoll: Orbis Books, 1978).

110. *Ibid.,* p. 57.

111. *Ibid.,* p. 165.

112. *Ibid.,* p. 43.

113. Clark Williamson, "Christ against the Jews: Jon Sobrino's Christology," unpublished manuscript, 1979, p. 13.

114. Jon Sobrino, *op. cit.,* pp. 205–206.

115. Clark Williamson, *op. cit.,* p. 16.

116. Leonardo Boff, *Jesus Christ Liberator* (Maryknoll: Orbis Books, 1978).

117. *Ibid.,* p. 284.

118. *Ibid.*

119. Carl G. Howe, *The Creative Era* (Richmond: John Knox Press, 1965), pp. 9–10.

120. R. Travers Herford, *The Aim and Method of Pharisaism,* republished as *The Pharisees* (Boston: Beacon Press, 1962).

121. Louis Finkelstein, *The Pharisees* (2 vols.) (Philadelphia: Jewish Publication Society, 1962).

122. Asher Finkel, *The Pharisees and the Teacher of Nazareth* (Leiden, Holland: Brill, 1964).

123. Michael Cook, "Jesus and the Pharisees—The Problem As It Stands Today," in *Journal of Ecumenical Studies* 15, No. 3 (Summer 1978), pp. 441–460.

124. J. Massingberd Ford, "The Christian Debt to Pharisaism," in *Brothers in Hope,* John M. Oesterreicher, ed. (New York: Herder & Herder, 1970), pp. 218–230.

125. Rosemary Ruether, "The Pharisees in First-Century Judaism," in *The Ecumenist* 11, No. 1 (November/December 1972), pp. 1–7.

126. Frederick Grant, "Paul the Pharisee," in *idem, Roman Hellenism and the New Testament* (New York: Charles Scribner's, 1962), pp. 132–147.

127. William E. Phipps, "Jesus, the Prophetic Pharisee," in *Journal of Ecumenical Studies* 14, No. 1 (Winter 1977), pp. 17–31.

128. Clemens Thoma, *op. cit.,* chapters 3 and 4.

129. Ellis Rivkin, "The Internal City," in *Journal for the Scientific Study of Religion* 5, No. 2 (Spring 1966), pp. 225–240; "The Pharisaic Background of Christianity," in *Root and Branch: The Jewish-Christian Dialogue,* Michael Zeik and Martin Siegel, eds. (Williston Park, N.Y.: Roth Publ., 1973), pp. 47–70; "The Meaning of Messiah in Jewish Thought," in *Union Seminary Quarterly Review* 26, No. 4 (Summer 1971), pp. 383–406; "Defining the Pharisees: The Tannaitic Sources," in *Hebrew Union College Annual* 1970, pp. 205–249; *The Shaping of Jewish History* (New York: Charles Scribner's, 1971); *A Hidden Revolution: The Pharisees' Search for the Kingdom Within* (Nashville: Abingdon, 1978).

130. Jacob Neusner, *The Rabbinic Traditions about the Pharisees Before 70* (3 vols.) (Leiden, Holland: Brill, 1971); *From Politics to Piety: The Emergence of Pharisaic Judaism* (Englewood Cliffs: Prentice-Hall, 1973); "The Use of the Later Rabbinic Evidence for the Study of First-Century Pharisaism," in *Approaches to Ancient Judaism: Theory and Practice,* William Scott Green, ed., Brown Judaic Studies 1 (Missoula, Mt.: Scholar's Press, 1978).

131. Josephus, *Antiquities,* XIII:171–173.

132. Ellis Rivkin, "The Internal City" (see note 129), pp. 230–231; cf. Mish*Aboth* 1, 1.

133. Ex. 20–24.

134. A succinct explanation of the significance of the Exodus covenant can be found in Roderick A. F. Mackenzie, *Faith and History in the Old Testament* (Minneapolis: University of Minnesota Press, 1965).

135. For more material on the Pharisees and armed revolution, cf. my article "Jesus and the Revolutionaries," in *The Christian Century* 89, No. 44 (December 6, 1972), pp. 1237–1241.

136. Stuart Rosenberg, "Contemporary Renewal and the Jewish Experience," paper delivered to the 1968 International Conference of Christians and Jews, York University, Toronto, Canada, Sept. 1968, p. 4.

137. *Ibid.,* p. 3.

138. Ellis Rivkin, "The Internal City" (see note 129), p. 236.

139. Stuart Rosenberg, *loc. cit.,* p. 6.

140. Albert Reville, as quoted in Jules Isaac, *Jesus and Israel* (New York: Holt, Rinehart & Winston, 1971), p. 44.

141. Jacob Neusner, *From Politics to Piety* (see note 130), p. 83.

142. *Ibid.,* p. 152.

143. Ellis Rivkin, *A Hidden Revolution* (see note 129), p. 310.

144. Cf. Claude Cuenot, *Teilhard de Chardin: A Biographical Study* (Baltimore: Helicon, 1965), p. 345.

145. Cf. Michael Cook, "Jesus and the Pharisees" (see note 123).

146. Cf. James Parkes, *The Foundations* (see note 40), p. 177; also, Chaim Raphael, "Jesus and the Jews," in *Commentary* 49, No. 6 (June 1970), p. 79.

147. Cf. the saying of R. Simon b. Menasiah, quoted in Jules Isaac, *Jesus and Israel* (see note 140), p. 60.

148. David Flusser, "A New Sensitivity in Judaism and the Christian Message," Part I, in *Encounter Today* 4, No. 4 (Fall 1969), pp. 123–131.

149. Michael Cook, "Jesus and the Pharisees" (see note 123), p. 455.

150. Ellis Rivkin, "Defining the Pharisees" (see note 129), pp. 240–241.

151. Michael Cook, "Jesus and the Pharisees" (see note 123), p. 457.

152. David Flusser, "A New Sensitivity in Judaism and the Christian Message," Part II, in *Encounter Today* 5, No. 1 (Winter 1970), p. 7.

153. S. G. F. Brandon, *Jesus and the Zealots* (New York: Charles Scribner's, 1967).

154. Cf. *Midstream* 16, No. 10 (December 1970), p. 65.

155. Joel Carmichael, *The Death of Jesus* (New York: Harper & Row, 1966).

156. Oscar Cullmann, *Jesus and the Revolutionaries* (New York: Harper & Row, 1970).

157. Cf. *Judaism* 20, No. 1 (Winter 1971).

158. John Howard Yoder, *The Politics of Jesus* (Grand Rapids: Eerdmans, 1972).

159. Etienne Trocmé, "L'Expulsion des Marchands du Temple," in *New Testament Studies* 15 (1968/69), pp. 1–22.

160. Albert Nolan, *Jesus before Christianity: The Gospel of Liberation* (Capetown RSA: David Philip, 1977).

161. *Ibid.,* p. 102.

162. *Ibid.*

163. Francis Fiorenza, "Critical Social Theory and Christology," in *Proceedings of the Catholic Theological Society of America* 30 (1975), pp. 109–110.

164. Cf. Josephus, *Wars,* 1.5.2.

165. Cf. William E. Phipps, "Jesus" (see note 127), p. 30.

166. *Ibid.,* pp. 30–31.

167. James Parkes, *The Foundations* (see note 40), p. 177.

168. *Ibid.*

169. Cf. Ellis Rivkin, "Defining the Pharisees" (see note 129), and Michael Cook, "Jesus and the Pharisees" (see note 123), p. 449n.

170. Shmuel Safrai and David Flusser "The Slave of Two Masters," in *Immanuel* 6 (Spring 1976), pp. 30–33.

171. David Flusser, "A New Sensitivity in Judaism and the Christian Message," in *Harvard Theological Review* 61, No. 2 (April 1968), p. 126.

172. Ellis Rivkin, "The Meaning of the Messiah" (see note 129), p. 391.

173. *Ibid.,* p. 401.

174. *Idem, A Hidden Revolution* (see note 129), pp. 307–308; cf. also "The Pharisaic Background of Christianity" (see note 129), pp. 48–49.

175. Rosemary Ruether, *Faith and Fratricide* (see note 8), p. 57. Cf. also "The Pharisees in First-Century Judaism" (see note 125), pp. 3–4.

176. Cf. John Pawlikowski, "The Historicizing of the Eschatological: The Spiritualizing of the Eschatological: Some Reflections," pp. 151–166; and Rosemary Ruether's response, pp. 243–246; in *Antisemitism and the Foundations of Christianity,* Alan Davis, ed. (New York: Paulist Press, 1979).

177. Raymond E. Brown, "Does the New Testament Call Jesus God?" in *Theological Studies* 26, No. 4 (December 1965), p. 546.

178. *Ibid.,* pp. 569–570.

179. Ellis Rivkin, *A Hidden Revolution* (see note 129), pp. 302–303.

180. *Ibid.,* pp. 307–308.

181. Cf. James A. Sanders, "An Apostle to the Gentiles," in *Conservative Judaism* 25, No. 1 (Fall 1973), pp. 61–63.

182. Cf. *Between God and Man* (Selected Writings of Heschel), Fritz Rothschild, ed. (New York: Free Press, 1959), p. 25. Cf. also Abraham Heschel, *The Prophets* (New York: Harper & Row, 1962).

183. Rosemary Ruether, in *Antisemitism* (see note 176), p. 246.

184. Letter by Teilhard de Chardin, of December 12, 1919.

185. Edward Schillebeeckx, *Christ, the Sacrament of the Encounter with God* (New York: Sheed & Ward, 1963), p. 151.

186. Cf. *Origins* 8, No. 40 (March 22, 1979).

187. Gregory Baum, "The First Papal Encyclical," in *The Ecumenist* 17, No. 4 (May/June 1979), p. 55.

188. *Ibid.*, p. 56.

189. A. Roy Eckardt, *Elder and Younger Brothers* (see note 22), p. 142.

190. For the biblical period, cf. chapter 5 of my *Sinai and Calvary: The Meeting of Two Peoples* (Beverley Hills: Benziger, Bruce & Glencoe, 1976), pp. 49–50. For examples of the modern discussion, cf. Irwin M. Blank, "The Covenantal People and the Righteous of All Nations," and William Cutter and Alan Henkin, "Universalism and Particularism: Where Ends and Means Collide," in *Journal of Reform Judaism* 26, No. 2 (Spring 1979), pp. 61–81.

191. Jacob Neusner, "Israel and the Nations," in *CCAR Journal* 17, No. 3 (June 1970), p. 31.

192. Tomaso Federici, "Study Outline on the Mission and Witness of the Church," in *SIDIC* 11, No. 3 (1978), pp. 25–33. This is the officially authorized English translation of Professor Federici's paper. (See also note 11.)

193. Abraham Heschel, *Israel: An Echo of Eternity* (New York: Farrar, Straus & Giroux, 1969), p. 124.

194. Manfred Vogel, "The Link Between People, Land and Religion in Modern Jewish Thought," in *SIDIC* 8, No. 2 (1975), pp. 15–32.

195. *Ibid.*, p. 29.

196. Walter Brueggemann, *The Land* (Philadelphia: Fortress Press, 1977), p. 185.

197. *Ibid.*, p. 187.

198. W. D. Davies, *The Gospel and the Land* (Berkeley: University of California Press, 1974), p. 367.

199. John Townsend, "Israel's Land Promises under the New Covenant," paper presented to the Israel Study Group, New York City, 1972.

200. Michael McGarry, *op. cit.* (see note 22), p. 93.

201. Eva Fleischner, *Judaism in German Christian Theology* (see note 61), p. 36.

202. My monograph, *The Challenge of the Holocaust for Christian Theology* (New York: Anti-Defamation League, 1978).

203. Jürgen Moltmann, "The Crucified God," in *Theology Today* 31, No. 1 (April 1974), p. 9.

204. *Ibid.*, p. 10.

205. *Ibid.*, p. 13.

206. *Ibid.*

207. A. Roy Eckardt, "Christians and Jews: Along a Theological Frontier," in *Encounter* 40, No. 2 (Spring 1979), p. 102.

208. *Ibid.*, p. 103.

209. Eugene Borowitz, *Contemporary Christologies* (see note 72), p. 92.

210. Irving Greenberg, "Lessons To Be Learned from the Holocaust," unpublished paper at the International Conference on the Church Struggle and the Holocaust, at Haus Rissen, West Germany, June 8–11, 1975.

211. Richard Rubenstein, *The Cunning of History* (New York: Harper & Row, 1978).

212. Douglas J. Hall, "Rethinking Christ," in *Antisemitism,* Alan T. Davies, ed. (see note 176), p. 183.

213. *Ibid.,* p. 182.

214. Franklin Sherman, "Speaking of God after Auschwitz," in *Worldview* 17, No. 9 (September 1974), p. 29. Cf. also Sherman's essay on the same theme, in *Speaking of God Today,* Paul D. Opsahl and Marc H. Tannenbaum, eds. (Philadelphia: Fortress Press, 1974).

215. *Ibid.,* p. 30.

216. Marcel Dubois, "Christian Reflection on the Holocaust," in *SIDIC* 7, No. 2 (1974), p. 15.

217. *Ibid.*

218. Clemens Thoma, *op. cit.* (see note 54), p. 159; cf. also p. 3.

219. Gregory Baum, "Catholic Dogma after Auschwitz," in *Antisemitism,* Alan T. Davies, ed. (see note 176), p. 142.

220. Francis Fiorenza, "Critical Social Theory" (see note 163), p. 106.

221. A. Roy Eckardt, "The Devil and Yom Kippur," in *Midstream* 20, No. 7 (August/September 1974), p. 68.

222. Cf. Uriel Tal, "Forms of Pseudo-Religion in the German *Kulturbereich* Prior to the Holocaust," in *Immanuel* 3 (Winter 1973/74).

223. For further discussion of this question, consult my *The Challenge of the Holocaust* (see note 202), pp. 5–17.

224. Cf. Balfour Brickner, "Christian Missionaries" (see note 9), pp. 37–41; also, "Christians Challenge the Rabbi's Response" (see note 10), pp. 42–46.

225. George P. Graham, "The Federici Paper: Some Reservations," unpublished paper.

226. Gregory Baum, "Catholic Dogma after Auschwitz" (see note 219), p. 138.

227. Tomaso Federici, *op. cit.* (see notes 11 and 193), IIa, par. 14.

228. *Ibid.,* III, par. 7.

229. Leon Klenicki, footnotes on paper by Tomaso Federici, in *Face to Face* (see note 11), p. 28.

230. Gregory Baum, "Rethinking the Church's Mission," pp. 113–128, and "The Doctrinal Basis for Jewish-Christian Dialogue" (see note 43).

Index of Authors

Stepping Stones to Further Jewish Christian Relations: An Unabridged Collection of Christian Documents, compiled by Helga Croner (A Stimulus Book, 1977).

Helga Croner and Leon Klenicki, editors, *Issues in the Jewish-Christian Dialogue: Jewish Perspectives on Covenant, Mission and Witness* (A Stimulus Book, 1979).

Clemens, Thoma, *A Christian Theology of Judaism* (A Stimulus Book, 1980).

Lawrence Boadt, C.S.P., Helga Croner, and Leon Klenicki, editors, *Biblical Studies: Meeting Ground of Jews and Christians* (A Stimulus Book, 1980).

STIMULUS BOOKS are developed by Stimulus Foundation, a not-for-profit organization, and are published by Paulist Press. The Foundation wishes to further the publication of scholarly books on Jewish and Christian topics that are of importance to Judaism and Christianity.

Stimulus Foundation was established by an erstwhile refugee from Nazi Germany who intends to contribute with these publications to the improvement of communication between Jews and Christians.

Books for publication in this series will be selected by a committee of the Foundation, and offers of manuscripts and works in progress should be addressed to:

Stimulus Foundation
785 West End Ave.
New York, N.Y. 10025

168